Dyes from Plants

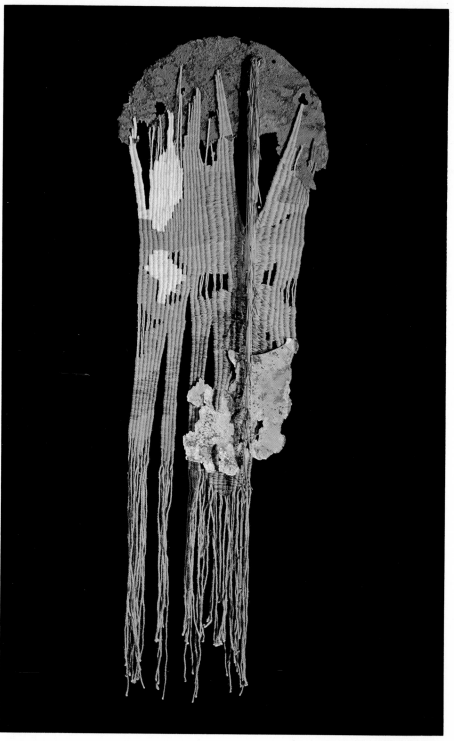

Frontispiece: A woven hanging inspired by the crescent shaped piece of rusty metal to which it is attached. The wool fibers were dyed to echo the colors of the metal, and a piece of old tin was incorporated. (Photo: Malcolm Varon, New York)

DYES FROM PLANTS

Seonaid M. Robertson

VAN NOSTRAND REINHOLD COMPANY

NEW YORK   CINCINNATI   TORONTO   LONDON   MELBOURNE

The following herbal illustrations are reproduced from *Handbook of Floral Ornament from Early Herbals*, Richard G. Hatton, Dover Publications, 1960: anchusa, apple, barberry, bilberry, broom, cherry, cotton, day lily, dog's mercury, dyer's weed, ivy, larch, marigold, Norway maple, poplar, ragwort, tansy, walnut. Indigo and logwood are reproduced from *History of the Vegetable Kingdom*, William Rhind, London, 1857. The balance of the illustrations, with the exception of those listed below, are reproduced or redrawn from *Theatrum Botanicum*, John Parkinson, London, 1640.

The following illustrations were drawn by Merle Nacht: big-bud hickory, black huckleberry, bloodroot, bracken, brasilwood, butternut, coreopsis, cutch, dahlia, goldenrod, hemlock, mahonia, mountain laurel, onion, osage orange, pokeweed, prickly-pear cactus, pyracantha, reeds, rudbeckia, silver birch, smartweed, snowberry, turmeric.

Madder was supplied by C.I.B.A., Basel, Switzerland.

Color illustrations 11 and 12 photographed by John Hunnex.

Color illustrations 1 through 7 are used by permission of *Everyday Art* magazine.

Van Nostrand Reinhold Company Regional Offices:
New York   Cincinnati   Chicago   Millbrae   Dallas

Van Nostrand Reinhold Company International Offices:
London   Toronto   Melbourne

Copyright © 1973 by Litton Educational Publishing Inc.
Library of Congress Catalog Card Number 73-178173
ISBN 0-442-26974-9

Designed by Visuality

Published by Van Nostrand Reinhold Company, A Division of Litton Educational Publishing, Inc., 450 West 33rd Street, New York, N.Y. 10001

16   15   14   13   12   11   10   9   8   7   6   5   4   3   2   1

Contents

Introduction

Men and animals share the earth with plants and are dependent on them. It was the spread of minuscule green organisms over the hard, starkly barren surface of the cold dead earth that prepared it to be the home of man millions of years later. These tiny organisms thrust powerful microscopic roots into the fissures of the rocks, breaking them up further; their creeping tendrils spread through the pockets of dust in the hollows, thus holding the particles together. As they died they provided humus for further generations of green to take root. Gradually, a green haze must have spread over the gray rock of the continents, and, over millennia, bigger and more complex plants developed and carpeted the valleys, holding moisture to feed more plants. Among these very early inhabitants of our globe was a fernlike tree of which we still have a miniature edition — the horsetail, which provides us with a greenish dye.

This basic interlocking of men and plants through food is as fundamental today as it ever was — for when we eat animals or birds or fish we are eating flesh that was, far back in the food chain, formed from eating plant life. We however are unlike most animals, some of whom, like the silkworm, subsist on one plant: one of the marks of our sophisticated life is the variety of our raw food. We eat many types of root vegetables and leafy vegetables, the unripe flowering heads of cauliflower and broccoli, the unripe seeds of peas and beans, ripening fruits both cultivated and wild, such as blackberries and wild grape. From many of these, whose intrinsic colors make them more appetizing, we also get a textile dye — as we do from the last two. Sometimes we color food with a different plant, for instance, rice with saffron — which also dyes fiber. Another mark of our sophistication is that we flavor and preserve our food with spices, and among those of the temperate zones, nasturtium and tansy also give good dyes.

We have made spirits and wines from all of the main staple foods — maize, rice, and wheat; then there are plants that are themselves mild stimulants, such as tea and coffee, both producing mild dyes. We have found medicinal plants with beautiful names, like sarsaparilla and ipecacuana, and plants that yield pain-killing drugs such as cocaine, long known to the Brazilian Indians, and hallucinatory drugs, such as hashish and opium. All these strangely differing properties men must have discovered from countless generations of experience.

The furniture in our homes is so familiar to us that we tend to forget that wood was once a growing plant and that men from primitives to pioneers have used it for the structure of their houses. Roofs are still thatched with reed or palm, while osiers and rushes have served for lightweight containers such as baskets and cradles. We are still relatively dependent on timber in building, and some contemporary architects, such as Alvar Aalto in Finland, have made a special feature of wood in domestic architecture, using its curves and grain with echoes of traditional ship-building techniques. We may admire the subtly different shades of cut wood ripening over the centuries in cedar shingles or rosewood furniture, but the dyes we get from wood — with the exception of brazilwood whose *heart* is the source of the historic red dye — usually come from the bark, as with logwood and fustic and our own apple, cherry, and birch.

It was only because plants offered men a floating, flexible substance that they were able to explore the water which bounded their lands. From the first hollowed-out log, the first papyrus boat on the Nile, to the timbered caravels that discovered the New World, from the osier coracle that brought Columba and Christianity to Scotland to the coracles still used in Ireland today, plants have carried men oceanwards to new experiences. The traditional range of European dyes, many of which are still used, was enormously extended by the discovery of dye-trees in Central America.

Ships that could sail the Atlantic — along with the growing science of navigation — opened up the dye trade of the seventeenth century, and supplemented the European range with the blue-purple of logwood and the red of brazilwood. The explorers found these great trees growing as natural forest, but from much earlier times, in Asia and Europe, plants have been cultivated specifically for their dye properties, especially indigo, madder, woad, and weld. One chapter of this book deals with cultivating a personal dye garden.

Other uses men have made of plants include bark cloth beaten thin and flexible, bark and raffia torn into thin strips for weaving and plaiting, jute and hemp twisted into cordage, and above all cotton and linen woven into cloth that was dyed almost as early as textiles were known.

Plants were also used in staining the skin. European aristocrats traveling incognito camouflaged their fair skin with walnut, and it is still one of our firmest dyes. The Romans who invaded Britain reported that the natives covered themselves for battle with a blue dye — almost certainly woad, still used by the occasional home dyer, and grown commercially for many centuries in Britain. Other plant dyes are used by New Guinea and South American natives today in traditional body patterns that identify them as one of their tribe.

The desire to beautify ourselves appeared early in human history, and palettes for cosmetics and the remains of rouge are found in early tombs. We know that Greek women dyed their hair with a plant called thapsus (*Thapsia asclepium*), which also dyed wool yellow, and buckthorn (*Rhamnus* species) was almost certainly used as a yellow hair dye.

Knowledge of dyes was probably handed down from mother to daughter and from wise woman to village flirt. In the English *New Herbal* of William Turner (Herbals were books of herbal remedies common from Elizabethan times) in 1551, we find of marigold: "Summe use to make theyr here [hair] yellow with the flowre of this herb not beyng content with the naturall colour which God hath given them." This leads us straight into the modern cosmetic industry, which still uses many vegetable salves and dyes. But of course the herbals are full of uses for plants in the borderland between cosmetics and medicine. For instance, the Anglo-Saxon Leechbook of Bald prescribes, "for sunburn boil in butter tender ivy twigs and smar therwith." There are also fascinating uses that lie between medicine and religion, such as fumigating with herbs, which is closely linked to the use of incense. Rituals in the gathering of herbs (such as the instruction to gather vervain with the left hand when neither sun nor moon is shining) survived from the worship of nature deities, in which so much of later science had its origin.

Trees and plants occur repeatedly in the myths by which men have sought to explain their life on earth. In Indonesia, where myths hold that men first grew from trees, the dead are returned to the branches of trees for burial. Among the Andamanese, a platform is erected in a tree and the body is placed there in burial — but only in the case of men dying in the prime of life. Trees were associated with oracles. The great oak of Dodona was constantly tended by priests, who slept beneath it. Most trees live longer than men do, so they seem natural receptacles of wisdom. The Buddha found enlightenment beneath the Bo tree, the Druids worshipped in groves — one could enlarge indefinitely!

Particular species of trees came to have symbolic meaning to different cultures. The Assyrian palm tree, constantly recurring in their art, was a symbol of vitalistic power related to the moon and the moon-goddess. The ancient Greeks decorated their vases and their temples with plant forms, especially the vine, and they danced at festivals with vine leaves in their hair. The vine, which lived on in the wine, was a symbol of indestructible life that passed into the Christian religion and persists in the Eucharist still: "I am the true Vine, drink of My blood." Some of the wild vines of American roadsides are suitable for wine and make a purple dye, so the plant has another form of perpetuation.

The Tree of Life was and is an archetypal symbol in innumerable cultures. Men have seen in the renewal of bare trees the hope of resurrection (as in the legend of Joseph of Arimathea, who thrust his thorn staff into the ground at Glastonbury and it continued to flower each year). Finally, when the tree has been cut down and the log trimmed, it may turn (as the myth of Osiris tells) into a coffin-boat to carry the body to new life on strange shores.

But the symbolism of plants and the use of them for dyes meet in a unique way in what are perhaps the most superb of all human artifacts — Persian carpets. "Paradise" is the Persian word for an enclosed garden, and in the cold days of winter the silky depths and rich patterns of the carpets hanging on the walls must have sustained their owners with a visionary hope until the trees came to blossom again. Our knowledge of earlier Persian gardens is obtained from the "garden carpets," which represent in plan not only the fountain in the center and the fretted walls but all the plants and trees, with loving precision. Here we can recognize the delicacy of the tulip, the carnation, and the rose, the boughs weighted with fruit, and the vigor of the waving cypress tree, the Persian symbol of eternal life, all knotted by human hands into a vision of paradise.

I have visited the Victoria and Albert Museum more times than I can count, but it was only on my last visit that I went specifically to look at and try to identify the dyes. On my way to the hall of Persian and Turkish carpets, I turned aside to pause momentarily in front of some of my favorite pieces — a fragment of a Peruvian shirt, some Coptic graveclothes, a medieval cope, an Elizabethan bedspread embroidered with spring flowers. Suddenly I was struck with wonder. I realized that almost all the marvelous colors in the acres of this rich museum were dyes from plants because, of course, chemical dyes were not invented until the mid-nineteenth century. How different would the whole place look if there were only the uncolored textiles! The art of extracting colors from plants has inspired men and women to weave patterns and embroider pictures that enrich life beyond telling.

In searching for wild plants or tilling the fields and tending cultivated ones, in learning their habits and properties, men have made yet one more link with the environment in which they live, learning to use it and to extract, without destroying it, that element of color which has so much enhanced their lives and still enriches ours.

1. Introduction to Dyeing

The commonest textile material in North America and Europe in earlier days was wool because the largest part of these areas is suitable for sheep-rearing. This is in contrast to India and much of Asia, where cotton and silk were more appropriate for wearing apparel, and where the climate was suitable for planting cotton and the mulberry bushes that feed silkworms. It is true that cotton flourishes in the southern states of the United States and that small quantities of silk are produced in the United States and Europe, but in both the traditional fiber is wool, and the plant dyes that were developed over the centuries by our forefathers were mainly for that fiber. So this book is chiefly concerned with dyes for wool, but a number of these will dye cotton and silk too, and some will dye some rayons. (A chapter is devoted to cotton dyes because some dyers will use cotton exclusively.) Some plants will dye raffia, dried rushes, and cane, used by the American Indians in weaving baskets and mats, and some will dye the porcupine quills loved by the Indians for decorating the pouches and garments that they still use on ceremonial occasions. Quillwork was largely superseded by beads, but some dye recipes from the Ojibwa, Menomini, Omaha, and others remain. When you are preparing a dyebath for wool, it is easy to throw in samples of all the fibers at hand to see how they react to that particular dye. Few synthetic fibers will take plant dyes, but some mixtures dye in an interesting way.

Wool can be dyed at many stages in the process of making a textile, starting with the fiber that can be gathered from hedges and barbed wire fences, or is bought or begged as a fleece or part of a fleece after shearing. If you buy even part of a fleece, it is worth trying to "separate" it, gently fingering and dividing the differing qualities, though to do this properly one has to be a professional of many years. But even an amateur can feel the difference between the coarse fiber of the rump and sides, the softer, shorter fiber of the belly, and the fine silky hairs under the chin. If these are kept separate they can be used for different purposes. Then again, each breed of sheep is different, and this is a fascinating study in itself.

The colors obtained from a plant will of course be more apparent on the common white wool, but dyeing on the mixed and dark natural wools also produces beautiful, subtle colors. Paula Simmons, in the state of Washington, dyes on all the natural browns of her husband's various breeds of sheep, producing a unique range of hand-spun wools.

PREPARING FIBERS FOR DYEING

If you dye wool as fleece, the scraps of dead herbage and thorns must be picked out, and natural grease in it must be removed by scouring. To enable the liquid to penetrate, the wool is lightly teased apart by repeated pulling outwards with both hands, and this soft mass is immersed in warm, lathery water. The water should be about hand-heat.

Soft water is much the best, and a rain butt, pool, or lake will provide this. (Soft water feels gentle to the skin and lathers well. Hard water, which contains lime compounds, gives a scum with soap substances, and when boiled deposits a powdery white dust on the bottom of the receptacle. In time this deposit builds up, forming a hard crust on kettles and pipes.) If only hard water is available, it can be softened by adding a few teaspoonfuls (depending on hardness) of acetic acid or, failing that, vinegar, to the gallon, or by using one of the commercial water softeners.

Soft household soap is still probably the best cleanser, and it is a good idea to put aside scraps of soap too small to use and heat them up with a little water to make jars of soft soap for this purpose. I have experimented in some dyes with the new biological, or enzyme, washing powders (to which some people are allergic) and have not found that they altered the colors much, but they might prove to do so in other cases. In a craft that depends so much on traditional knowledge, one might as well stick to the traditional soft soap until something else is proved better.

Steeping and moving the fleece around lightly in plenty of water, rather than real washing and squeezing, will prevent matting. Thorough rinsing in clear soft water is essential, and then the wool can be spread out to dry on a clean sheet, or dyed.

Not all of us can obtain wool in the fleece and have the fun of spinning or tufting it, and most of my students have begun with hanks of wool from Woolworth's or with old part-hanks of knitting wool stored somewhere in the house. It does not matter what the thickness or ply of the wool is, or whether it is plain or fancy. For early experiments you can use old white knitted garments, unraveled, washed and wound into skeins. In fact, it is a good idea to put into the dyebath, in the early experiments, different types of wool, thereby building up a stock of varieties in one color from which to choose when you come to embroider or weave. Different types and mixtures of fibers will take the same dye in slightly different ways and so produce a quantity of similar but varied shades. Many "wools" now have an admixture of man-made fiber to prevent shrinking, and these strands may not take plant dyes or take them only slightly. Wool with any oil in it must be scoured like fleece. All wools should be gently washed in soapsuds and very well rinsed before dyeing.

Dyeing can also be done at the stage of the finished cloth, but to dye a quantity of cloth evenly takes skill. The beginner will rather prefer to find out first which plants do give dyes, and so build up a vocabulary of color. So, the experiments here call for wool fiber, shop-bought or homespun or in the fleece.

To prevent skeins from getting tangled up in the dyebath, it is customary to tie them loosely in one, two, or three places, according to whether they are very short skeins of embroidery length or longer knitting skeins. (It is not possible to dye balls: the dye does not penetrate to the center, so wool obtained this way must be rewound in skeins.) Always tie the skeins loosely or the dye will not get through and you will produce a "tie-dye" effect unwittingly. After knotting the tie-thread to itself, leave one long end to hang over the edge of the pot — pull the skein up by it to see how the dye is taking. This is for small skeins; heavier ones are better threaded on a tape that is looped over the pan handles or to a cord above.

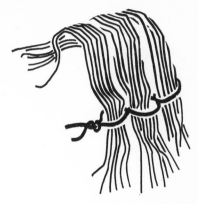

A hank or skein tied up for the dyebath.

EQUIPMENT

The absolute minimum of equipment for dyeing can be found in any kitchen, or can be bought cheaply secondhand; the serious dyer will collect his special items later. My greatest pleasure has come from dyeing in the open air, especially near a lake or pool providing soft water, with a few bricks for a fireplace and a line strung between two trees.

Vessels. For beginning experiments you will need one or more large boiling pans, preferably of unchipped enamel (often known as "agate" or "marbled").

The best vessels for both dyeing and mordanting are steel, which does not affect the color and is easy to clean. But steel is expensive, and enamel (so long as it is not chipped, because the iron underneath will affect the color) or aluminum or galvanized iron can be used. Brass, copper , and iron vessels may act as mordants (discussed in Chapter 2) and will modify the dye color.

The largest vessel that can be easily lifted is desirable. The minimum size is a 1-gallon container for 4 ounces (120 grams) of wool; one that holds 1½ gallons is better.

In addition to the pans, some pails (plastic, enamel, or galvanized iron) are necessary.

Rods. For stirring, unbreakable stainless steel (cut from lengths of rod or fine tubing) again is the ideal material, but glass rods are also excellent. For beginners, lengths of dowel rod, peeled smooth sticks, or even the long handle of a wooden spoon will serve. Wood will absorb some dye, however, so a different stirrer must be used for each color.

If the rods have a bent end, they will not slip into the dyebath. Glass rods can be easily bent at home by heating in a hot flame. If you use dowel rods, drill a hole in the end, thread a wire through, and bend it to hang on the rim or handle of the pan of dye.

A sieve made of a nylon-stocking toe stretched over a frame of twisted wire.

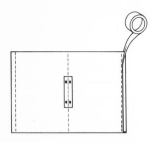

A page being prepared for a record book. The edges are bound with clear tape, and the center is reinforced with tape. The broken lines indicate where folds are to be made.

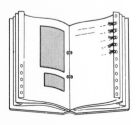

The page in the record book. One side holds the actual plant, dried, in a plastic bag, and/or a sketch or photograph of the plant in its habitat. Below this are details of its habitat. Opposite are brief notes about mordant, dyeing time, date, etc. Dyed samples are knotted through the holes at the edge of the page. By this method one can keep the samples folded inside the book so they will not get dirty, but turn out the folded flap to have the relevant colors hanging out of the book when needed.

Sieves. A steel or cheap plastic kitchen sieve is best for straining, but muslin or a nylon stocking stretched on wire as illustrated will serve. (Old stockings are fine to hold the plant material too, and I just throw the whole lot on the compost heap together, which saves a lot of cleaning up.)

A means of heating. For the first experiments, you can use the kitchen stove, a camp cooker, or even a low fireplace. But when you come to handle larger quantities, the height of a kitchen stove is awkward, and one or more gas rings (bottled gas is suitable), electric rings, or hotplates at a lower level are convenient. An old household wash-boiler is excellent. I just put a few bricks together in the shed and use an old galvanized bath resting on them, with a pail below the water butt to be warmed for rinsing, and a line hung above to save carrying. In the kitchen, spread plastic or paper on the floor.

Water. You need plenty of soft water for the dyebath, at least a gallon to 4 ounces (120 grams) of wool. Rain water is best, soft lake or river water good. Hard water can be softened with zeolite (a natural mineral product marketed under various trade names, such as Calgon). In a hard-water district more soap and *more of the dyestuff* are needed. Cotton does not need to be treated quite so gently as wool in dyeing, so if only a smaller vessel is available, a little less water can be used. Few beginners want to invest in baths large enough to hold the minimum 4 gallons to dye or mordant a pound of wool or cotton.

A line to dry on is necessary. It is also useful to have some means of stretching wool skeins — giving them a gentle pull and turn from time to time — while they are drying. If they are dried on a dowel rod hung on two hooks instead of on a line, this gives something to pull against, but many common household articles, such as a sleeve board, will also serve.

A record book and tie-on or clip-on labels are important. If recipes are written out, a tiny label can simply bear the number of the recipe; or a larger one can bear the plant name and part, the date, time cooked, and mordant if used. A useful method of keeping a record of all colors obtained, even with the tiniest remnant, is illustrated here.

Measures. For weighing, a pair of household scales and letter scales or an old chemical balance that measures quarters of an ounce and pounds or grams and kilos will serve the dyer's purposes. For volume, measuring cups with fluid ounces marked off and the standard American measuring spoons* (use flat, not heaped, spoonfuls) are needed. For small quantities a measuring cup or test tube marked with ½ and 1 fluid ounce is also needed. Pour a gallon of water into a large bucket and paint a line for a rough ½-peck measure and add another gallon and another line for 1 peck: this is a useful measure for volume when you are working with bulky plant material.

British cups and spoons come in all sizes, but American ones are standardized and can be purchased cheaply. A table of equivalents for the dyer's use is given on page 16 and at the back of the book.

When you use a chemical or letter balance, it is important to keep it on a flat surface and not to put the chemicals straight on the pan. The proper way is to cut two squares of paper together from newspaper and put one on each pan (so

*Obtainable in Britain from Harrods, Knightsbridge, London.

A student's record book.

that the same weight is added to each side). Then put weights and chemical on the pieces of paper; lift the chemical on the paper.

Thermometers. You will need a dairy thermometer or a household thermometer with waterproof markings, and preferably long enough to reach near the bottom of the dyebath. Either Fahrenheit or Centigrade will do; both are given here.

A wringer is a great help when you dye or mordant large quantities of fiber.

Many people will want to wear a pair of *rubber gloves,* and I carry *plastic bags* and *rubber bands* on all country excursions to bring home dye material I find. Small pieces of *muslin* or old *nylons stockings* are used to make sieves or for dyeing by the simultaneous method described later in this chapter.

Do not be put off by this list of equipment, which is for serious dyers. Begin with what you have in your own kitchen on the basic recipes, and build up gradually.

TABLE OF MEASURES

Weight

1 ounce (oz) equals 28.349 grams (g), and 1 pound (lb) equals .453 kilograms (kg), but for our purposes the following rough equivalents are practical:

1 oz = 30 g
½ lb = 250 g
1 lb = .5 kg
2 lb = 1 kg

It is only in the measurements of chemicals that one needs even this degree of accuracy. Whenever possible, measures are given in American teaspoons (tsp) or tablespoons (tbsp) as well.

Volume

The British gallon, or Imperial gallon, contains 4 Imperial (40-ounce) quarts; the American gallon contains 4 quarts of 32 ounces each. I have found this to be just enough for dyeing 4 ounces of wool, but Americans should use a generous gallon. The British cup is 10 fluid ounces; the American is 8 fluid ounces. Because American and British liquid measures are different, I have tried to avoid using fluid ounces and multiples thereof. I have, where possible, used teaspoons and tablespoons, and so give their fluid-ounce equivalents here:

1 tsp = 1/6 fl oz (1 European coffee spoon)
1 tbsp = ½ fl oz (1 European soup spoon)
2 tbsp = 1 fl oz

For dry measure, I have given quantities in quarts (qts) and pecks (pks); the difference between the American and British is so slight that I have not distinguished between them.

I have totally ignored the metric liters, but for the convenience of dyers using the metric system, the following equivalents may be used:

1 fl oz = 30 cc
1 gal = 4½ liters
1 qt (dry measure) = 1 liter
1 pk = 9 liters

GENERAL INFORMATION FOR THE DYER

The following terms are often used rather loosely so I define them as I have used them:

Cold — cold to the touch, anywhere between 32° and 40° Fahrenheit (written °F.) or 0° and 5° Centigrade (written °C.).

Hand-heat — a little warmer than body temperature, but comfortable to the touch, roughly 100°–120°F. or 38°–49°C.

Simmering — the temperature at which there is a slight continuous movement on the surface, but few bubbles bursting, roughly 180°–200°F. or 82°–93°C.

Boiling — temperature at which water in every part of the liquid is briskly bubbling and turning into steam, 212°F. or 100°C.

The common practice in dyeing is to put the plant parts into cold, soft water and heat slowly. All plants should be washed before use, as dirt or chemical sprays may affect the color.

Berries are crushed or set aside in a warm place to "draw" their juice before they are entered in the bath.

The dye substance is usually extracted while the temperature of the bath is rising from cold to about 180°F. (82°C.), and you must always begin from cold and not hurry this stage.When the water is at the simmer—that is, just below boiling point—lower the heat and simmer for the time specified in the recipe. It is a useful general rule that barks need long simmering or even boiling; fresh leaves and flowers need shorter, gentler treatment.

A lid is not necessary, but it will prevent the steam and any smell from escaping. (The exception to this is with chrome, which will be discussed in Chapter 2.) If much water boils away, make the bath up to the original amount with boiling water. Stir the bath frequently with a clean rod. When the dye has been extracted, strain off the plant remains and throw them away, and return the liquor to the pan.

When the liquor is cool or at hand-heat, the clean, thoroughly wetted fiber is entered. The fibers must be *clean* and *wet*, or the dye will take unevenly: many dyers always wash wool in soapy water and give it a final rinse in cool water just before dying.

WASHING FIBERS

Steeping in soapsuds as described on page 12 is sufficient for slightly soiled wool, but wool with oil in it or unraveled wool may need two or three steepings. Whip soft soap or good soapflakes into a lather in hot water, and allow it to cool to hand-heat. Immerse the wool and move it gently about a little rather than scrubbing it; it may be left in until the water is cold. Rinse the wool thoroughly in tepid water and squeeze it gently or put it through a wringer at light pressure. Wringing or twisting it will felt the wool and make it take the dye unevenly.

Since the wool has to be wet when put into the dyebath, it can be kept wet after washing if it is to be dyed within days. If not, then it must be thoroughly wetted again. The best way to do this is to steep it overnight or for a few hours in a bath of warm water and take it out to squeeze gently or put through a light wringer ½ hour before dyeing. The wool can then be laid on a clean cloth while the dye is prepared, which will help the dampness to spread evenly. As fisherman and hill-climbers know, to their satisfaction, it is very difficult for water to penetrate wool completely — the outside may appear soaked, but the center resists the wet. The problem this useful quality presents to dyers can only be overcome by really thorough soaking. When it is dried, wool regains much of its resilence, and we appreciate its rain-resistant property.

DYEING

Wool and wool mixtures must be entered into *cold* water — that is, less than hand-heat. Cotton can be put into a hotter bath and is usually boiled rather than simmered. With silk thread, rapid boiling may tangle the fibers, so it is best to

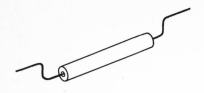

A simple roller made from dowel rod and wire.

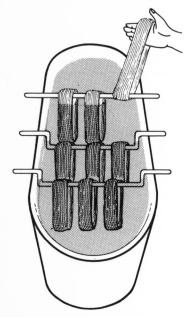

Dyeing in an old-fashioned bath tub. This shows how the skeins on rollers are "worked" in the dyebath. With the bent rods, all the fiber is kept immersed.

dye it under about 200°F. (93°C.). It is a question of balancing the treatment of the fiber with getting the strongest, fastest dye possible.

During the dyeing, the fiber must be "worked" or moved about to dye evenly. This can be done by gentle stirring, but with a large quantity of fiber it is better to hang it on rollers or bent rods as illustrated. You can make rollers of cut broom handle and roll them along the side of the bath to move the wool, but this way all the wool is not immersed all the time. Bent steel rods or hollow wooden rods with wire through them allow you to move the wool around easily.

When the fiber is ready to be removed, lift it out on a rod and let it drip over the bath for a few moments. This way the temperature is reduced gradually, and you do not waste the dye or flood the rinse water with it.

RINSING

To rinse the fiber, have two or three pails of soft, clean water at hand—one hot, one hand-heat, and the third cold. Rinse the fiber in each pail, squeezing the water out over the pail. A wringer at light pressure can be used for large quantities. Treat wool gently to preserve its soft, fluffy texture; cotton can be treated a little less carefully.

Most colors get lighter as they dry, but a few continue to develop even after the fiber has been taken from the dyebath. Fastness is often increased by leaving the fiber in the dyebath to cool for as long as overnight, but this also darkens or dulls the color. Sometimes the fiber is steeped in a chemical such as common salt to deepen or set the color. This is called an *afterbath*.

LABELING

After thorough rinsing, as described above, the fiber should be labeled. It may then be hung on the twigs of a handy tree in the breeze, or on a line, or on a wall with drip papers underneath, or — best — on a rod supported by two hooks at an open window over a sink, but *never* in direct sunlight until it is dry and set. The rod enables you to hook your finger through the skein and give a gentle stretch, especially good for wool, as the fiber dries. The ties made to keep the skein from unraveling in the bath may be left on if it is to be dyed in another color. A short length should be entered in your record book with a short description of the process used and the source of the plant.

The essential steps in dyeing with plants may be summarized as follows:

(1) Prepare the dyebath by heating the plant material in soft water until the dye is extracted.

(2) Strain off the plant material, discard it, and return liquor to the pan.

(3) Cool the liquor to hand-heat or cooler.

(4) Enter the clean, thoroughly wetted fiber tied in skeins.

If you want to save time in experiments, put the plant substance into the bath tied loosely in a bag made of muslin or an old nylon stocking and heat to extract

1
A group of autumn dyes. These skeins of wool were dyed with elder, tansy ragwort, walnut, blueberry, onion, and other plants.

3
These colors were obtained from various lichens.

4
A range of colors obtained from onion skins and walnut hulls.

2
Wool dyed with madder, weld, walnut, and goldenrod.

5
Wool dyed with walnut hulls.

the dye. During the last ½ hour, put the fiber into a pan of cool water alongside the dyebath and heat it slowly. Then the fiber can be transferred quickly to the dyebath to simmer together with the plant material for the required time.

(5) Bring bath to the simmer and simmer the fiber for the required time, moving it gently about from time to time.

(6) Remove the fiber on a rod and let it drip for a few moments over the dyebath.

(7) Rinse several times, preferably first in hot water, then in water at hand-heat, then in cold water. After each rinse, squeeze the fiber gently to remove excess water.

(8) Label.

(9) Hang in the shade to dry.

THE SIMULTANEOUS METHOD OF DYEING

In the case of plants that suffer with too much cooking (especially fragile flowers and leaves and often plants that yield reds and yellows), it is better to put the bag of plant material *and* the fiber into the cold bath at the same time and bring them to the simmer together. I call this the simultaneous method of dyeing.

Because this book is intended to be used by beginners and those who are interested in testing many plants for dyes, the quantities given in the recipes are small. It is much easier to multiply for larger quantities of fiber than to divide for smaller ones. Most people in their early days of plant dyeing will not want to work with the pounds of wool usually referred to in dye books, but with small quantities for embroidery, toy-making, or experimental weaving rather than for lengths of cloth. So, the recipes in this book are for 4 ounces (120 grams) of fiber. Small tests can be done with a quarter of the amounts given in the recipes, using 1 ounce (30 grams) or small scraps of fiber—as in the five experiments following. In such tests, the amount of dyestuff need not be quite exact, as the color will vary anyway according to season and locality, but chemicals should be measured as precisely as possible. The small quantities used in fun experiments are not easy to repeat exactly—but plant dyeing never is!

Four ounces of fiber need at least 1 gallon of water (more is better); 1 ounce needs at least ½ gallon and preferably more. The essential ratio is that of dye substance to fiber—the amount of water used is mainly to allow the yarn to move freely in the bath. Since the amount of dye substance in any batch of plants varies with the season, the ground, the past weather, and so on, I advise using rather larger quantities of plant material than are generally suggested, because many new dyers are disappointed in the result when the color looks weak and thin. The quantities I give will seldom exhaust the dye substance in the liquor, and a fresh batch of fiber heated in the same bath will take the dye as a weaker color (the second or third dyeing of fresh fiber is called an "exhaust bath"), but these quantities do give more certain results.

If the dye is not exhausted, the liquor may be stored in tightly capped glass jars for some time, depending on the climate and the particular plant. The liquor can be kept indefinitely in a refrigerator.

Five Experimental Recipes

To provide beginners with some first experiences of making color from plants, I have chosen five simple substances, in the belief that one or more of them will be readily available whether the dyer is a town or country dweller, and no matter what the locality and season of the year. The five are black walnut hulls, apple or pear bark, bilberry or blueberry (also, depending on where you live and which species is dominant, called whortleberry, farkleberry, deerberry, cowberry, rabbiteye, or huckleberry), onion skins, and turmeric, a common household spice.

These are all non-mordant dyes and do not require fixing. However, most households have cream of tartar (potassium acid tartrate) and perhaps alum (potassium aluminum sulfate). With a small quantity of dyestuff to test, a pinch of alum with an even smaller pinch of tartar, or the tartar alone, added to the bath just before the test fiber, will usually strengthen the color. Mordanting is dealt with in Chapter 2.

Experienced dyers may skip the remainder of this chapter, which aims at giving some immediate results by simple means.

TO MAKE PINK TO PURPLE FROM BILBERRY OR BLUEBERRY
Vaccinium species

Method: Crush the berries in the bottom of a pan and add rather less than ½ gallon soft water, because the juice contributes liquid. (In this case it is especially important to use soft water — rain water or water from the peaty pools near where the shrubs are found. If soft water is not available, add 1 tablespoon of vinegar.) Bring to the simmer, then simmer for ½ hour. Strain off the berries and discard them, and return the liquor to the dyebath. When it has cooled to hand-heat, enter the clean, thoroughly wetted wool. Slowly bring the bath to the simmer and simmer gently for 30 minutes, stirring lightly to move the wool about. Remove a skein and hold it to drip over the dyebath for a few moments. Rinse the wool in hot soft water and squeeze gently; then rinse in cooler water and squeeze gently again. Label the skein and hang to dry in the shade. The wool will probably be heather pink.

1 OZ (30G) OR LESS WOOL, DIVIDED ROUGHLY INTO FIVE SKEINS AND TIED WITH STRING OR THICK THREAD

½-1 LB (250G-.5KG) OR ABOUT 2 HANDFULS BILBERRIES OR BLUEBERRIES, FRESH, CANNED, OR DRIED

½ GAL OR LESS SOFT WATER FOR THE DYEBATH

Continue simmering the wool still in the bath for another 30 minutes, and remove a second skein. Rinse, label, and dry as before.

Simmer remaining wool in the bath for another hour and remove another skein, which should be much darker in color than the first two, and continue as before until all the wool has been dyed.

Soaking the wool after it comes from the dyebath in a solution of 1 tablespoon salt to a gallon of water makes the color more blue, but also grays it a little.

Dyers often use the simultaneous method described on page 20 with bilberries or blueberries because it gives a purer color.

21

TO MAKE SHADES OF BROWN FROM BLACK WALNUT HULLS

Juglans nigra is even better than the English *J. regia*

1 oz (30ɢ) or less wool, divided roughly into five skeins and tied

10-20 black walnut hulls or husks, picked fresh when developing dark spots, picked rotten from the ground, *or* picked earlier and stored in jars of water

½-1 gal soft water for the dyebath

Method: If the hulls are freshly picked or dried, they will benefit from steeping at least overnight in soft water. Then simmer them in this water, made up to ½ or 1 gallon, for 1 to 2 hours. Strain off the hulls and discard them, and return the liquor to the dyebath. When it has cooled to hand-heat, enter the clean, thoroughly wetted wool. Slowly bring the bath to the simmer and simmer gently for 30 minutes, stirring lightly to move the wool about. Remove a skein and hold it to drip over the dyebath for a few moments. Rinse the wool in hot soft water and squeeze gently; then rinse in cooler water and squeeze again. Label the skein and hang it to dry in the shade.

Continue simmering the wool still in the bath for another 30 minutes, and remove a second skein. Rinse, label, and dry as before.

Simmer remaining wool in the bath for another hour and remove another skein, which should be much darker in color than the first two, and continue as before until all the wool has been dyed. By top-dyeing the darker skeins (as described in Chapter 6), you can make a strong black.

It is also possible to get a brown dye from the *bark* of the black walnut tree: follow the recipe for apple and pear bark.

The pale brown inner shells of shop walnuts do yield a dye, but it is infinitely less powerful than that of the outer shells or husks.

TO MAKE SOFT YELLOW FROM APPLE OR PEAR BARK

Malus species and *Pyrus* species

1 oz (30ɢ) or less wool, divided roughly into five skeins and tied

½-1 lb (250ɢ-.5ᴋɢ) apple or pear bark, from recently cut branches or fallen trees if possible

½-1 gal soft water for the dyebath

Method: Chop the bark roughly and simmer it in the soft water for 1 to 2 hours. The color yielded by bark usually becomes stronger the longer it is simmered, up to 3 or 4 hours, so this liquor can be simmered quite briskly before the wool is entered. If much of the water boils away, make it up to ½ or 1 gallon. Strain off the bark and discard it, and return the liquor to the dyebath. When it has cooled to hand-heat, enter the clean, thoroughly wetted wool. Slowly bring the bath to the simmer and simmer gently for 30 minutes, stirring lightly to move the wool about. Remove a skein and hold it to drip over the dyebath for a few moments. Rinse the wool in hot soft water and squeeze gently; then rinse in cooler water and squeeze gently again. Label the skein and hang it to dry in the shade.

Continue simmering the wool still in the bath for another 30 minutes, and remove a second skein. Rinse, label, and dry as before.

Simmer remaining wool in the bath for another hour and remove another skein, which should be much darker in color than the first two, and continue as before until all the wool has been dyed.

TO MAKE YELLOW FROM ONION SKINS

Allium cepa

Method: Put the skins in the soft water and bring to the simmer, then simmer for ½ to 1 hour. A lid will prevent the smell from escaping. If much of the water boils away, make it up to ½ or 1 gallon. Strain off the skins and discard them, and return the liquor to the dyebath. When it has cooled to hand-heat, enter the clean, thoroughly wetted wool. Slowly bring the bath to the simmer and simmer gently for 15 minutes, stirring lightly to move the wool about. Remove a skein and hold it to drip over the dyebath for a few moments. Rinse the wool in hot soft water and squeeze gently; then rinse in cooler water and squeeze gently again. Label the skein and hang it to dry in the shade.

Continue simmering the wool still in the bath for another 15 minutes, and remove a second skein. Rinse, label, and dry as before.

Simmer remaining wool in the bath for another 15 minutes and remove another skein, which should be much darker in color than the first two, and continue as before until all the wool has been dyed.

The addition of any of the mordants given in Chapter 2 to this recipe will produce a brassy yellow to orange. While in the western United States I repeatedly got a fine lime green from the skins of red onions, and again in Pennsylvania from imported Italian red-onion skins. It is possible that other red onions give this, but I have not been able to obtain it from Texan red onions nor from onions imported into Britain.

1 OZ (30G) OR LESS WOOL, DIVIDED ROUGHLY INTO FIVE SKEINS AND TIED

2 HANDFULS OUTER SKINS OF COMMON YELLOW ONIONS

½-1 GAL SOFT WATER FOR THE DYEBATH

TO MAKE YELLOW FROM TURMERIC

Curcuma longa

Method: Put the turmeric powder in the soft water and stir well while bringing to hand-heat. Enter the clean, thoroughly wetted wool. Slowly bring the bath to the simmer and simmer gently for 2 minutes, stirring lightly to move the wool about. Remove a skein and hold it to drip over the dyebath for a few moments. Rinse the wool in hot soft water and squeeze gently; then rinse in cooler water and squeeze gently again. Label the skein and hang it to dry in the shade.

Continue simmering the wool still in the bath for another 2 minutes, and remove a second skein. Rinse, label, and dry as before.

Simmer remaining wool in the bath for another few minutes and remove another skein, and continue as before until all the wool has been dyed. Ten minutes will give a brilliant yellow.

Although turmeric needs no mordant, chrome and tin as described in Chapter 2 will both give interesting colors. The yellow can also be used for top-dyeing with walnut (see Chapter 6). Turmeric is a very strong, brilliant dye, but it does not last well over the years.

If not every one of the first experiments you do is completely successful, they will at least give you confidence that ordinary plants can yield permanent, varied dyes. Now you will want to understand more of the process of dyeing and go on to experiment with mordants.

1 OZ (30G) OR LESS WOOL, DIVIDED ROUGHLY INTO FIVE SKEINS AND TIED

1½ TSP TURMERIC POWDER

½-1 GAL SOFT WATER FOR THE DYEBATH

2. Mordants

It has been shown that certain plants will dye without any further substance being present (these are known as "substantive" dyes, but I shall continue to use the simpler term, "non-mordant" dyes). Quite often, a plant that yields a non-mordant dye, such as bilberry or buckthorn, will give a stronger color *with* a mordant and often a range of colors with different mordants. The lichen dyes, discussed in Chapter 7, are the main class of non-mordant dyes that give a range of color without any chemical.

The word "mordant" comes from the French *mordre*, to bite, and mordants can be described as metallic salts with an affinity for both fibers and dyestuffs, which improve the color fastness. Dyes that need a mordant are sometimes called "adjective" or "indirect" dyes.

The Chinese had dye-workshops as early as 3000 B. C.; the first Western dyers known were the primitive Lake Dwellers of what is now Switzerland, who lived about 2000 B. C. But the first certain use of *mordants* was in the Middle Kingdom in Egypt (between about 2200 and 1500 B. C.), as is known from textiles found on mummies preserved by the dry air of the Egyptian tombs.

We cannot be sure what were the sources of the early mordants, but we can guess from what was available and from the knowledge we have from some areas of the world still using "primitive" methods today. In the remote parts of Brazil I found wood ashes used, as they still are in Peru. The early American colonists are recorded as using "salt, vinegar, soda, cream of tartar, or 'lye.'" "Drip lye" was made at home from wood ashes, and "chamber lye" (urine) was a ready source of ammonia and other salts. Urine was until recently and may still be used in Ireland, Scotland, and many parts of Europe. Male urine was sometimes said to be better than female! Sumac galls and oak galls were both used as mordants as well as dyes. The galls on the leaves are caused by an insect whose attack stimulates the tree to excessive growth. A brown ball that serves as the insect's home is formed; the insect will be found on cutting through a gall. Tannin, which is concentrated in the galls, is the mordant.

American Indians used what was to hand as mordants. The Ojibwa used local clays, grindstone dust, the water in which iron had rusted, and wood ashes. Many of the plants they used were unrecorded, but we have this account of a Navajo woman preparing to dye wool brown with mahogany root bark*: "She uses juniper ash water for her mordant. . . .She sets fire to a big handful of juniper branches, burning only the green needles, and holds them over a frying pan so that the ashes will fall into it. Then she adds boiling water, which after straining, she uses as a mordant with the mahogany root bark."** The mordant seems to have been added to the dyebath after the solids were strained off. Two parts water to one part green needles, by volume, were used.

In Bali the ashes of coconut-palm leaves were strained through a bamboo sieve, mixed with cold water, and used as a mordant for the beautiful Turkey-red dye from madder; the Hebridean dyers recently used roots of sorrel with meadowsweet to make a kind of blue.

Beginning dyers have a number of mordants already around the house — salt, vinegar, several forms of soda, cream of tartar, and possibly wood ashes. Some others, such as sorrel, sumac, and oak galls, may be found readily in the countryside.

In addition to adding substances to a bath for mordanting, the vessel that is used may itself serve as a mordant. From many parts of the world come reports of dyers who use copper or tin vessels to brighten colors, and an iron kettle or iron filings to dull them. The use of an aluminum vessel — or the addition of a piece of sheet aluminum to a dye-pot with a little soda — is advocated by a New Zealand dyer*** as an alternative to alum mordant. The beginning dyer, however, should do the first experiments in a steel or enamel pot, or the "basic" color of the dyes will not be apparent.

The most common chemical mordants used by plant dyers are listed below, but alum is the most generally helpful, and no one should be put off beginning to dye by the absence of the others.

Alum (potassium aluminum sulfate), which is used in building construction as well as household preserving, comes in white crystals. You may be offered aluminum ammoniate, which will serve, but the sulfate is better especially for frail plants. Raw alum, which occurs as soft white chunks in the flat Indian country of the United States, especially around sulfur springs, in New Mexico, is used by the Navajo for mordanting light, pure colors. They use it cold, but also throw chunks onto the fire and add them foaming to the boiling dyebath.

Cream of tartar (tartaric acid) is the white crystalline powder familiar as an ingredient in baking. It is often used in conjunction with alum.

Chrome (potassium dichromate) is used by photographers, and comes in

*This is obviously not the mahogany tree, which does not grow in Navajo country, but it has been suggested that it might be *Cerocarpus*, which is known as mountain mahogany.
**Nonabeh G. Bryan, *Navajo Native Dyes*, 1940.
***Joyce Lloyd, *Dyes from Plants of Australia and New Zealand*, 1971.

orange crystals. It is sensitive to light and must be kept in a dark jar, preferably in the dark, especially when in solution. It is also called bichromate of potash.

Tin (stannous chloride) comes in off-white crystals and should be stored in a dry place.

Iron (ferrous sulfate), also known as copperas and green vitriol, comes in soft green crystals that are corrosive when damp or in solution.

Blue vitriol (copper sulfate) comes in beautiful blue crystals and is a useful mordant for green dyes. It is a poison.

Glauber's salts (sodium sulfate) is useful for extracting the last of the color from an exhaust bath, and for obtaining an even dye, but it sometimes darkens colors.

Other common chemicals used in dyeing are:

Washing soda (sodium carbonate), another white crystalline powder often used for household cleaning. It is sometimes called sal soda.

Common salt (sodium chloride) and *vinegar* (a weak solution of acetic acid).

Oxalic acid is corrosive and should not be handled with the fingers. It comes in white crystals that should be stored and labeled accordingly. Alternatives are given in recipes that call for oxalic acid.

Lime (calcium oxide), is a chemical commonly used for building and in gardens.

Alum, Glauber's salts, and probably blue vitriol can be bought at any pharmacy. Potassium dichromate, stannous chloride, and ferrous sulfate may be found in most school laboratories or ordered from a dyehouse or chemicals supplier, who can also supply the other chemicals listed more cheaply than pharmacies. Chrome may be obtained from photographic suppliers. (A list of suppliers is given at the back of the book, but dyers may find that the less common substances are not always sold in quantities of less than a pound. Since the amounts required by dyers are very small, an individual might share with a club, school, or other group.)

Some of the chemicals listed here are harmless, but some are dangerous. All should be kept stoppered and labeled and away from children.

When a chemical is added at some stage during the course of dyeing, the fiber should always be lifted out of the bath and the chemical stirred in well before the fiber is returned to the bath.

PREPARATION OF FIBERS FOR MORDANTING

When wool or cotton is mordanted, the fiber must be tied up in some way to prevent it from getting tangled while being moved about in the bath. The traditional way is to tie it as for dyeing, as described on page 13. The ties must not be too tight, or the mordant will not penetrate under them, which does not appear until the dye color shows up unevenly.

The fibers must also be clean or they will not accept the mordant evenly, and again the dye color will take unevenly. Directions for washing are given on page 12.

I mordant a quantity of fiber at one time, and it may be months before I use it, so I have a system of using different fibers to tie up the skeins so that they

need no further marking until dyed. Any easily available string will do, but I tie those for alum mordant with cotton embroidery thread, those for chrome with cotton string, those for tin with nylon string, and those for iron with fine twine. Any number of refinements could be made — two knots for alum plus tartar, and so on.

Wool to be dried and kept for a long time should be moth-proofed, or be stored in mothproof bags.

PROCEDURE

In many cases it is possible to add the mordant to the dyebath, but sometimes the smallness of the quantities is a problem. I am always testing plants in whatever country I am, and I would never be put off doing this by not having any ready-mordanted wool — I simply add a few crystals of alum and tin (which I normally carry in tiny bottles) to a small quantity of the plant liquor to see if it is worth investigating further. However, on the whole it is easier and more exact to mordant separately, and to keep a supply of small hanks of both cotton and wool ready-mordanted for testing. On the other hand, when you see that the color of the dye needs to be modified, you can add cream of tartar or tin near the end of the dyeing to brighten it, or iron to dull or "sadden" it.

It is convenient to mordant quantities of different types of wool or cotton and cotton mixtures and fancy threads at one time. But since the dye recipes in this book are for 4 ounces (120 grams) of fiber, the following mordant recipes are for the same quantity, and the amounts can be multiplied as necessary.

Mordants For Wool

TO MORDANT WOOL WITH ALUM AND CREAM OF TARTAR

Method: Mix the alum and cream of tartar with a little boiling water and add to the rest of the water. Stir to dissolve the chemicals well, and heat. When the water is about hand-heat, enter the clean, thoroughly wetted wool. Slowly bring the bath to the simmer — this should not take less than 1 hour — stirring occasionally; then lower the heat and simmer the wool (1 to 1½ hours for coarse wool, ¾ to 1 hour for fine wool). Stir gently from time to time. Remove the wool with a rod and hold it to drip over the pot for a few moments. When it is cool enough to handle, gently squeeze out the excess water, but do not wring the wool or rinse it. Dye the wool immediately, or keep it damp in a cloth or bag for the next day, or dry and store it for future use.

Different results are obtained by the use of alum alone or cream of tartar alone, but the combination is usually more successful. When alum is given as the mordant, alum and cream of tartar is to be understood.

4 OZ (120G) WOOL, TIED IN SKEINS

1 OZ (30G) OR 1¾ TBSP OR SLIGHTLY LESS ALUM
¼ OZ (7G) OR 1½ TSP CREAM OF TARTAR

1 GAL SOFT WATER

TO MORDANT WOOL WITH CHROME

4 oz (120G) WOOL, TIED IN SKEINS

⅛ OZ (3.5G) OR A SCANT ½ TSP CHROME
(TOO MUCH WILL DARKEN THE COLOR)

1 GAL SOFT WATER

Method: Mordanting with chrome is best done just before dyeing. Dissolve the chrome in a little boiling water and add to the rest of the water. Stir to dissolve the chrome well, and heat. When the water is about hand-heat, enter the clean, thoroughly wetted wool. Put a plate or other weight on top of the wool to keep it submerged and *cover the pot with a lid* except when stirring. Chrome is very sensitive to light: if light falls on any part of the fiber, it will darken it and cause uneven dyeing. Slowly bring the bath to the simmer; then lower the heat and simmer the wool (1 to 1½ hours for coarse wool, ¾ to 1 hour for fine wool). Stir gently from time to time. Remove the wool with a rod and wrap it in a towel. When it is cool enough to handle, gently squeeze out the excess water, but do not wring the wool or rinse it. Keep the wool wrapped in a towel even for the moments between mordanting and dyeing if it is dyed immediately. It can be kept damp in the towel for the next day, or dried and stored in the dark for future use.

Chrome gives wool a soft and silky texture, making it pleasant to handle.

Sometimes adding cream of tartar to the dyebath will improve the colors obtained with chrome-mordanted fibers. For 4 ounces (120 grams) of wool, add 3/16 ounce (6 grams) cream of tartar to the dyebath before entering the wool, and stir well to dissolve it.

TO MORDANT WOOL WITH TIN

4 oz (120G) WOOL, TIED IN SKEINS

⅛ OZ (3.5G) OR A SCANT 1 TSP STANNOUS CHLORIDE CRYSTALS

⅛ OZ (3.5G) OR A GENEROUS 1½ TSP CREAM OF TARTAR
OR
⅛ OZ (3.5G) OR 1 TSP OXALIC ACID CRYSTALS

1 GAL SOFT WATER

Method: Heat all but a little of the water to hand-heat and then stir in the cream of tartar or oxalic acid, dissolved in a little boiling water. When this is thoroughly dissolved, stir in the tin, dissolved in a little more boiling water. Keep the bath at hand-heat and enter the clean, thoroughly wetted wool. Slowly bring the bath to the simmer — this should not take less than 1 hour; then lower the heat and simmer the wool (1 to 1½ hours for coarse wool, ¾ to 1 hour for fine wool). Remove the wool with a rod and hold it to drip over the pot for a few moments. Do not leave the wool in the bath longer than necessary, as it will be roughened. Wash the wool in warm soapy water and rinse in warm water.

To prevent brittleness, after dyeing tin-mordanted fiber is usually washed again in soapy water and rinsed thoroughly.

Tin is also used to brighten reds (which may have been mordanted with another mordant); this is called "blooming." For 4 ounces (120 grams) of wool, add ½ teaspoon tin, dissolved in a little boiling water, to the dyebath 20 minutes before the dyeing is finished.

6

These three groups of wool have been dyed with the same plants–blackberry, pokeberry, goldenrod, and walnut–but the group at top left was mordanted with tin; the group at top right with chrome, and the group at bottom with alum.

TO MORDANT WOOL WITH BLUE VITRIOL

Method: Dissolve the copper sulfate in a little boiling water and add to the rest of the water. Stir to dissolve it well and heat. When the water is about hand-heat, enter the clean, thoroughly wetted wool. Slowly bring the bath to the simmer — this should take not less than an hour — stirring occasionally; then lower the heat and simmer the wool (1 to 1½ hours for coarse wool, ¾ to 1 hour for fine wool). Stir gently from time to time. Remove the wool with a rod and hold it to drip over the pot for a few moments. When it is cool enough to handle, gently squeeze out the excess water, but do not wring the wool or rinse it. Dye the wool immediately, or keep it damp in a cloth or bag for the next day, or dry and store it for future use.

If mostly bright colors are desired, 1½ teaspoons cream of tartar may be added at the beginning of the bath.

4 OZ (120G) WOOL, TIED IN SKEINS

¼ OZ (7G) OR 2 TSP CRUSHED COPPER SULFATE CRYSTALS

1 GAL SOFT WATER

TO MORDANT WOOL WITH IRON

Method: The most common method is to dye first and then remove the wool (holding or handing it over the bath in the steam to prevent it from cooling) and add the iron and cream of tartar to the bath. Stir thoroughly, return the wool to the bath, and simmer for 20 to 40 minutes, according to the depth of color desired. As iron always dulls the color (but produces some fine somber greens from yellow dyes), this is called "saddening." Rinse especially thoroughly after mordanting with iron.

Mordanting beforehand can be done by following the method just given for tin, with the amounts of ferrous sulfate and cream of tartar specified here.

The same effect can also be obtained by dyeing in an iron vessel.

Note: Silk should not be mordanted with iron.

4 OZ (120G) WOOL, TIED IN SKEINS

⅛ OZ (3.5G) OR 1¼ TSP FERROUS SULFATE

¼ OZ (7G) OR 2¼ TSP CREAM OF TARTAR

1 GAL SOFT WATER

Silk is usually mordanted like wool. Recipes for mordanting cotton and linen are given in Chapter 5.

One of the fascinations of using mordants is a certain underlying *quality* of color that is conveyed to the shades fixed by one mordant, as though they were in one musical key.

Alum is not dramatic in its effect, but it is the most widely used and the most stable, and will often improve the brightness and fastness of colors that can be obtained from non-mordant dyes. Too much alum makes wool sticky.

Chrome gives a warm underglow to many colors and brings out reds and oranges, but mutes greens into a grayish green. It softens the texture of wool. It is extremely light-sensitive. Too much darkens wool.

Tin brightens most colors, and you can get startling brassy effects that can glow when crossed in weaving with darker colors. Too much tin makes wool rather brittle and harsh to touch.

Iron always dulls — or, in the dyers' language, "saddens" — colors, and it is usually a constituent of blacks. Too much iron hardens wool.

Burning leafy or woody plants, as every gardener knows, produces potash, but the varying concentrations of chemicals at different times of the year in different tree-trunks or roots, or dead fruits (or the tannin in oak galls) results in complex mixtures of compounds. The study of them is analogous to that of the potter who uses ash glazes: it has been found undeniably that the ash of, say, beech-wood burned in the autumn of a certain wet year will differ not only from the ash of oak-wood but from that of beech in other years and with different weather.

In addition to the basic mordants discussed, washing soda, lime water (water solution of calcium hydroxide), and potash (potassium carbonate) or the ashes from any wood fire are all worth trying. Many yellow dyes — coltsfoot, bog myrtle, heather — will turn green on adding iron, in the form of water in which iron filings have rusted, or ferrous sulfate crystals. This both changes and fixes the color. The same mordant will modify the tan color from acorns to a warm gray. Copper sulfate — those crystals of deep turquoise color — produces a warm brown from dock leaves rather than the normal yellow, and, on the other hand, turns an exhaust bath of the lichen *Parmelia* from red-brown to soft green.

Unless you are going to go into mordants in a very scientific way, only tradition, built up over generations, is any guide. As amateur dyers — in the true sense of the words, lovers of dyeing — we must accept the uncertainties, the disappointments, with the delights, and *enjoy* rather than deplore the magic that we cannot completely explain.

3. Dyeing in Every Season

In whatever situation, in whatever season, and no matter if the environment is rural or urban, there will be dye plants to be found. The first thrustings of green in spring often produce yellow to green dyes, such as those from bracken fronds or lily-of-the-valley leaves, and one can pull up the rogue weed, dog's mercury, for the dye-pot with aggressive satisfaction. In high summer when flowers are prolific the range of color is wide and again in autumn the berries provide not only food for us and the birds but many dyes as well. When the plants have died down, those whose roots contain dye can be dug up with even less misgiving (though sometimes these root dyes are better gathered in summer) while the faded foliage remains to identify them. (Or you can mark the spot with a stick in summer with an eye to later collection.) Even when winter comes and the earth is bare, there are the lichens to be scraped off the rocks — this is best done when it is damp, and one dyer has worked chiefly with lichen dyes in the Arctic. When the earth is quite frozen, the foliage and berries withered, and the plant roots sealed away from us by snow, the barks remain. One is not usually allowed to pick plants in city parks, but the trees and shrubs have to be clipped, and these clippings and remaining berries, or the dead leaves of poplar and other trees, can be collected. But much of the fun of plant dyeing is to extend one's range and get into the country to look for plants that yield a dye. For this and other reasons I have arranged the recipes in this chapter according to the seasons.

OBTAINING DEPTH AND VARIETY OF COLOR

There are three main ways of obtaining color of some strength: using a large amount of the plant in proportion to the yarn to be dyed; boiling for a long time;

and leaving the dyed wool to steep in the liquor after boiling. The last two may cause delicate colors to be dulled. But in almost all cases, stronger color will be obtained with a mordant.

As will become apparent, different colors are obtained under apparently the same conditions from the same plant when it is growing in different soils, when the season has been exceptionally wet or dry, or when it is gathered at different times of the year. I am told that at Penland School of Handicrafts in North Carolina, twelve different shades were obtained in the twelve months of the year from the leaves of just one plant, the rhododendron.

For all these reasons, it is seldom possible to match a batch of dye exactly, so in planning a large piece of work it is essential to dye enough of each color at one time. If two different shades of one dye need to be matched, the two lots can be simmered for 15 to 30 minutes in a bath containing 1 cup of Glauber's salts to each gallon of water.

COLOR FASTNESS

Fastness of color may be expressed as fastness to light and fastness to washing. Few plant dyes can claim to be absolutely fast over many years, but they do fade to beautiful soft colors, very different from some harsh or vapid chemical dyes. All the recipes given in this book offer some degree of fastness unless otherwise noted, and the dyes with a long history, such as weld, indigo, and madder, a good degree. Obviously, the use to which the dyed fiber is to be put will be a factor. We do not expect wool embroidery to be washed frequently, and many woven and knitted objects would be dry-cleaned. Many subtle colors not very fast to washing, such as pokeberry, can be used for wool embroidery, therefore. On the other hand, bedspreads are perhaps better washable, and curtains must have fastness to light, so it is wise to choose cotton dyes for bed linen and eschew dyes from barks for curtains, since dyes made from barks rely on tannin, and will darken with exposure to light. It is for these reasons that mordants are so often used, but to disprove the idea that plant dyeing is complicated and lengthy, I suggest beginning with no mordants or only such as are common household substances.

GENERAL PRINCIPLES FOR DYEING WITH FLOWERS

Flowers are best gathered fresh and used straight away. Simmer them briefly (between ten minutes and an hour), or the delicacy of the color will be lost. I take out a sample every 20 minutes or so and stop when the required color is reached. Often large quantities of flowers are needed. If it is not important to get an even color throughout the wool (such varied effects give a sparkle to embroidery, for instance), then you can put the fiber in with the flowers, so the simmering time will be quite short. You can put the flowers in a muslin bag or nylon stocking to prevent them from getting tangled in the wool.

Liquor from the strained flowers will seldom keep. Some flowers, such as forsythia, can be dried by tossing in the warm shade, but most flowers dye much better when fresh, and when the weather is hot, I carry a stoppered jar of water and pick them straight into it, pouring this directly into the dyebath.

If not enough blossoms of one type are available on any day, you can make a mixture of those that give similar colors — for instance, marigolds, dahlias, coreopsis. Or fustic or turmeric may be added to a yellow flower dye to give it brilliance.

GENERAL PRINCIPLES FOR DYEING WITH BERRIES

Most berries are best when gathered just overripe and used straight away. But purplish red shades can be varied by keeping the berries in a warm place until they ferment, or, in some cases, letting them almost rot. Hard berries should be pounded with a wooden club or, failing that, with a hammer to free the juices.

Some berries, such as elder and sloe, can be stored dry in glass jars for future use if no dampness clings to them. Again, if the liquor made from them is strained and stored, it should be sealed like jam or kept in a very cold place to prevent fermentation.

It is possible to dye with canned or bottled berries — which occasionally, as with blackberries, give a stronger color — and often with dried berries (such as bilberry or blueberry) or with frozen berries, but on the whole the best results are from fresh ones.

For drying, spread the berries on a wire mesh tray (a cooling tray for baking will serve) and gently shake it each day or so until they shrivel. The important thing — unless they are being deliberately fermented to obtain a different color — is that no moisture should remain on them. When they are dry, store them in a porous (not airtight) container such as muslin bags or old stockings, preferably hung in a dry place. Label them.

GENERAL PRINCIPLES FOR DYEING WITH BARKS

Tree barks are used for preparing leather hides because they contain tannin. Because of the tannin content, colors from barks come out yellow to brown, sometimes a warm red-brown. Many trees will be found with lichens or mosses growing on the bark and these may affect the color, so it is wise to avoid such parts and to wash bark in warm water before using it.

Great care should be taken in removing bark from forest trees. The living part of a tree is the circle between the bark and the trunk, from which the tree increases its girth inwards and stretches the bark to increase it outwards. Therefore, to rip off the bark down to the living cells is destructive to the tree. I have not found much difference between the color obtained from living trees and *recently* felled trees, so obviously it is better to take the bark from cut trees or from a recently broken branch if these are available. But when trees grow too large—and this is useful to know in one's gardening—their growth can be slowed down by "bark-ringing." This means cutting the bark down to the living ring in an *almost* complete circle in acute cases, or in two half-circles about four inches apart to slow growth only moderately. Afterwards seal the wound with lead paint or wax compound. (Do not cut the bark down to the living ring in a complete circle—this will kill the tree.)

OF LEAVES OF HERBS, OR TREES

1. Of leaves choose only such as are green and full of juice; pick them carefully, and cast away such as are declining, for they will putrify all the rest. So shall one handful be worth ten of those you buy in Cheapside.

2. Note what places they most delight to grow in, and gather them there; for betony that grows in the shade is far better than that growing in the sun, because it delights in the shade; so also such herbs as delight to grow near the water, shall be gathered near it, though haply you may find some of them upon dry ground. The treatise will inform you where every herb delights to grow.

3. The leaves of such herbs as run up to seed are not so good when they are in flower as before, (some few excepted, the leaves of which are seldom or never used) in such cases, if through ignorance they were not known, or through negligence forgotten, you had better take the top and the flowers than the leaf.

4. Dry them well in the sun, and not in the shade, as the saying of the physician is; for if the sun draw away the virtues of the herb, it must needs do the like by hay, by the same rule, which the experience of every country farmer will explode for a notable piece of nonsense.

5. Such as are astrologers (and indeed none else are fit to make physicians) such I advise; let the planet that governs the herb be angular, and the stronger the better; if they can, in herbs of Saturn, let Saturn be in the ascendant; in the herb of Mars, let Mars be in the Mid-heaven, for in those houses they delight; let the Moon apply to them by good aspect, and let her not be in the houses of her enemies; if you cannot well stay till she apply to them, let her apply to a planet of the same triplicity; if you cannot wait that time neither, let her be with a fixed star of their nature.

6. Having well dried them, put them up in brown paper, sewing the paper up like a sack, and press them not too hard together, and keep them in a dry place near the fire.

7. As for the duration of dried herbs, a just time cannot be given, let authors prate at their pleasure; for,

1st. Such as grow upon dry grounds will keep better than such as grow on moist.

2dly. Such herbs as are full of juice will not keep so long as such as are dryer.

3dly. Such herbs as are well dried, will keep longer than such as are slack dried. Yet you may know, when they are corrupted by their loss of colour, or smell, or both: and, if they be corrupted, reason will tell you that they must needs corrupt the bodies of those people that take them.

4. Gather all leaves in the hour of that planet that governs them.

Culpeper's *Herbal*

In most recipes the best color is obtained from the inner bark, as with black oak and cherry. Barks should be cut into pieces and soaked overnight. All barks need to be simmered for a long time, perhaps two hours, but the liquor can usually be stored in jars after it has been sieved. If no dark cupboard or opaque jars with lids are available, cover glass jars with tents of aluminum foil or with brown paper bags.

All barks and certain other parts of plants, as noted in the recipes, can be dried for future use. Bark dried in the air or in a slightly warm oven can be stored in boxes or drawers; label it at the time. In this way the prodigal days of summer and autumn can be used in gathering and storing up material for winter use or for when there is time to deal with it in a leisurely way.

GENERAL PRINCIPLES FOR DYEING WITH LEAVES

Tender green leaves, like nettle, bracken fronds, spinach, should be picked and used immediately or the clear green will tend to go yellow-brown. Do not overheat them or the same thing will happen. Some tougher leaves such as birch are better soaked for 24 hours before simmering, and very tough leaves can be macerated before soaking. When you use the whole top of a plant, or leaves that are more mature, such as dock or Lombardy poplar, it is better to cut them up, but in fact I seldom do this unless the plant is big — I just bend and crack them with my hands.

Some leaves, such as those of weld, can be gathered whole, tied by the stems, and hung in a warm place to be chopped up later for the dyebath. Leaves taken from trees should be stripped off the branches, which contain tannin and would dull the color.

On the whole, the best time to take leaves is when they are just mature but before seeding, and this is especially important in the case of weld if you want a fresh green.

We cannot do better than take the advice of Culpeper for gathering leaves (see extract).

¾ TBSP ALUM

1½ TSP CREAM OF TARTAR

SCANT ½ TSP POTASSIUM DICHROMATE

SCANT 1 TSP STANNOUS CHLORIDE

1½ TSP CREAM OF TARTAR

2 TSP COPPER SULFATE

1¼ TSP FERROUS SULFATE

2½ TSP CREAM OF TARTAR

My students find it easy to use the principles by thinking of their dye material as "tough" or "tender." "Tenders" are fragile flowers or leaves, to be used fresh and simmered briefly. "Toughs" are barks, roots and nuts to be chopped, probably soaked, and simmered at length.

The seasonal recipes have been reduced to the essentials for brevity. A detailed description of the procedures for dyeing has been given in Chapter 1. In all the following recipes, it is presumed that the wool will have been previously mordanted as described in Chapter 2. If the wool has not been mordanted, add the mordant to the dyebath, in the quantity given here, before entering the fiber, and stir well to dissolve. The exception is iron: it is added near the end of the dyeing so as not to harshen the wool unnecessarily.

Recipes For Spring

SWEET GALE OR BOG MYRTLE
Myrica gale

This 1½-to 5-foot-high bush with long grayish leaves of a very distinctive scent grows in bogs and waste places with acid soils. It is a feature of the moors of Scotland and Scandinavia, where it has been used for centuries for a yellow dye, and is also native to North America. It is one of the plants that make a good dye when the leaves are gathered green in late spring or early summer and dried for winter use. Avoid the woody stems, as they will dull the color.

4 OZ (120G) OR 1-2 QTS LEAVES, DRIED OR FRESH

Mordant: Alum gives a good yellow. Myrtle will do with 1½ times the usual amount of alum. The additional alum can be added to the dyebath.

½ OZ (15G) OR ¾ TSP ALUM

Method: If you use dried leaves, they should be steeped overnight in the water to be used for dyeing. If the leaves are fresh, put them in cold water and heat slowly. Simmer for 1 hour. Strain off the leaves and cool the liquor. Add the alum. Enter the clean, wetted wool and return bath to the simmer. Simmer for ¾ to 1 hour, according to the depth of color desired. Rinse the wool twice and dry.
   Dagmar Lunde of Norway suggests an afterbath of copper to get a warm yellow-brown, or an afterbath of iron to get a yellow-green.

AGRIMONY
Agrimonia eupatoria

A yellow flower of the rose family, agrimony grows in spikes 1 to 3 feet high, with nine pinnated saw-edged leaves rising from saw-edged whorls on the stem. The fruits carry little hooks that catch on passing animals and serve to disperse the seeds. A common plant in northern Europe in grassy places, this agrimony is sometimes found wild in eastern North America. No doubt it was brought to the U.S. by early colonists for medicinal purposes. It is also known as "church steeples" and sticklewort.
   It was formerly used to treat snakebite, and the flowers were put in lemonade to cure colds.
   The fragment agrimony (*Agrimonia odorata*) can also be used for dyeing. It has larger, paler flowers and grows in the shade in acid soils.

1 LB (.5 KG) OR ABOUT 2 QTS LEAVES AND STALKS, FRESHLY CHOPPED

Mordant: Alum gives yellow, chrome gives gold.

Method: Put leaves and stalks in cold water and heat slowly. Simmer for 1 to 1½ hours. Strain off the plant material and cool the liquor. Enter the clean, wetted wool and return bath to the simmer. Simmer for about 1 hour. Rinse the wool twice and dry.

Elsie Davenport, an English dyer, says that agrimony gathered in Devon gave orange.

OAK

Black Oak — *Quercus velutina* formerly known as *Q. tinctoria*
Red Oak — *Q. borealis*
White Oak — *Q. alba*
English Oak — Q. *robur*

The oaks are distributed widely over the temperate and subtropical parts of Europe and North America, and the family is too well known by its acorns to merit detailed description here. The black oak is distinguished by downy twigs and hairy buds; the leaves are dark green and glossy above, pale and downy below. The red oak has hairless twigs and leaves that are dull green above and downy below, with brown hairs in the vein axils. The acorn cup is very shallow. The leaves of the red oak turn red in autumn, whereas the white oak turns purple and the English and black oak turn soft brown.

The black, white, and red oak are common in the United States. The black oak is not indigenous in Britain, and while the red is found in parks and gardens, the English or common oak is native, and was formerly much planted to provide the timber for ships and houses.

The dye is obtained from the inner bark, which was stripped and prepared into an extract (that from the black oak being called quercitron), especially in the mid-eighteenth century. The black oak extract was used in a complicated recipe with other substances to give black, or more simply yellow to orange, while the extract from red oak produced yellows, and that from white oak gave browns. Quercitron can still be bought from dye houses.

Dyers using fresh bark should strip it from felled trees and take out the soft inner bark. I have boiled it fresh, but it is more ofted dried and powdered. I have had much better colors from red and black oak, but the English oak is a stand-by for browns.

The oaks will also dye silk, and a recipe for cotton is given on page 93.

Mordant: Oaks need no mordant to make buff-browns because of the tannin in the bark, and oak galls can also be used without a mordant to produce brown if they are pounded with a hammer. Alum, gives yellow, chrome gives gold, and on silk tin gives orange.

Method: Put the bark in cold water and heat slowly. Simmer for 1 to 1½ hours. Strain off the bark and cool the liquor. Enter the clean, wetted wool and return bath to the simmer. Simmer for 1 hour. Rinse the wool twice and dry.

Prolonged boiling brings out the tannin and dulls the brighter colors.

1 LB (.5 KG) FRESH BARK
OR
¼ OZ (7 G) EXTRACT

NETTLE

Urtica dioica

The common nettle, which is too well known as a garden weed and which is used as a vegetable in some European countries, will yield a soft greenish yellow dye. It is a real satisfaction to make some use of this pernicious intruder, but those who can keep their gardens free of it will find plenty in the hedgerows. It is easily identified — it gave rise to the following verse by the seventeenth century poet Aaron Hill:

Tenderhearted stroke a nettle
And it stings you for your pains
Grasp it like a man of mettle
And it soft as silk remains

But I still prefer to wear gloves!
The fresh green tops are best for dyeing.

Mordant: Alum gives yellow-green, iron gives gray-green.

Method: The simultaneous method of dyeing is preferable here. Put the tops in a mesh bag (the bulk will be reduced quickly when the nettles are in the bath) and enter in the bath together with the clean,wetted wool. Slowly bring bath to the simmer and simmer wool and nettles for ½ to ¾ hour. Lift the bag out of the bath frequently and work the wool to keep the dyeing even. Rinse the wool twice and dry.

1½-2 PKS OR ABOUT A PAILFUL FRESH NETTLE TOPS

BRACKEN OR BRAKE

Pteridium aquilinum

A common coarse fern reaching 4 or more feet high, bracken is distributed over most of the globe in waste places. When young, it is distinguished by its coiled fronds like wrought-iron work or curled fingers, and when older by its stiff harsh stem. The best dye is obtained from the young fronds just as they are unfolding, but I have obtained good color right up to August by using only the top 6 inches or so. I have read that the roots make a black dye, but I have not been able to obtain this. The same shoots do make a good gray dye for silk.

Mordant: Alum gives yellowish green, chrome gives a rich, warm lime green.

Method: If you use tops, put them in cold water and heat slowly. Simmer for ¾ hour. If you use young shoots, only steep them in hot water for 1½ to 2 hours instead of simmering. Strain off the shoots or tops and cool the liquor. Enter the clean, wetted wool and bring bath to the simmer. Simmer for ¾ hour. Rinse the wool twice and dry.

2 LBS (1 KG) YOUNG SHOOTS OR TOPS OF OLDER PLANTS

38

LILY OF THE VALLEY

Convallaria majalis

A low-growing, rapidly spreading garden flower that produces a famous scent, lily of the valley loves shade and throws up its spikes of scented white bells in spring. The leaves are good for yellow dye from spring right through summer, until they begin to turn yellowish, when they give a bronze gold. In order not to reduce the garden stock, I often wait until July, when the leaves have had a chance to feed the rhizomes. The plant multiplies so quickly, however, that what you use will be replaced. Silk can be dyed by the same recipe as wool.

Mordant: Alum gives soft to gold yellow, chrome gives a strong warm gold, almost bronze, with autumn leaves.

Method: Soak the leaves overnight before using or chop and put them fresh into cold water. Heat slowly and simmer for ½ to ¾ hour. Strain off the leaves and cool the liquor. Enter the clean, wetted wool and return bath to the simmer. Simmer for 20 minutes, 40 minutes, or 1 hour, according to the depth of color desired. Rinse the wool twice and dry.

If a pinch of lime is added to the bath before entering the alum-mordanted wool, the color tends toward a pale, soft apple green.

½ LB (250G) OR ½ PK LEAVES

A PINCH OF LIME (OPTIONAL)

BLOODROOT

Sanguinaria canadensis

This flower of rich woods and shaded banks is found in North America from Nova Scotia to Manitoba and Nebraska and south to Florida. It is grown in British and American gardens for its graceful flowers. From the swollen roots or rhizomes rise on single stems fan-shaped leaves of five to nine lobes and white flowers, with eight to sixteen long petals, that bloom in April and May. The petals fall quickly, but the plant can be recognized in summer by its fruit, a capsule about an inch long, pointed at both ends.

The dye was used by the Indians and is probably what the Ojibwa used to dye porcupine quills red. Fresh root was used to color wooden implements yellow. I have had no opportunity to dry the roots, but as soon as the plant in my garden has increased, I shall experiment with this. Dried roots are available from some herb houses.

Mordant: Alum gives red-orange, tin gives pinkish reds.

Method: The simultaneous method of dyeing is preferable for bloodroot. Cut the roots into small pieces and soak overnight or at least a few hours in the water to be used for dyeing. Then put the pieces in a mesh bag and enter together with the clean, wetted wool. Slowly bring bath to the simmer and simmer wool and roots ½ to ¾ hour. Lift the bag out of the bath frequently and work the wool to keep the dyeing even. Rinse the wool twice and dry.

5-6 OZ (150-180G) OR 2 ROOTS, FRESHLY CUT

DOG'S MERCURY

Mercurialis perennis

This is a slightly hairy upright perennial that grows to a foot in height from small rhizomes. It is common in shady woods and hedges and as a garden weed in Britain. The tiny green male and female flowers grow on separate plants, and the pollen is wind-borne. It is one of the few plants that flourish in beech woods. Dog's mercury can only be used young; after spring is over it gives a dull color.

Mordant: Alum gives yellow.

Method: The simultaneous method of dyeing is preferable here. Put the plant in a mesh bag (the bulk will be reduced quickly when the plant is in the bath) and enter together with the clean, wetted wool. Slowly bring bath to the simmer and simmer wool and dog's mercury for ½ to ¾ hour. Lift the bag out of the bath frequently and work the wool to keep the dyeing even. Rinse the wool twice and dry.

1-1½ PKS OR ABOUT A PAILFUL OF THE WHOLE PLANT, CUT OFF ABOVE GROUND WITH SHEARS OR SCISSORS AND CHOPPED ROUGHLY INTO 1- OR 2-INCH LENGTHS

HEMLOCK

Western Hemlock — *Tsuga heterophylla*
Common or Northern Hemlock — *T. canadensis*
Southern Hemlock — *T. caroliniana*

The hemlocks are trees of temperate North America, especially the Pacific coast for western hemlock, but now planted extensively in Britain. The western hemlock was introduced into Britain in the mid-nineteenth century by John Jeffrey for the Oregon Association of Edinburgh, which was formed to further the introduction of Pacific-coast trees. Queen Victoria wanted it to be named after her late husband. The graceful eastern hemlocks are mostly grown for their beauty. Judiciously pruned, they also make superb hedges.

The hemlocks are large evergreens with small cones rather like larch cones but pendant, not erect. The bark, which is the part used for dye, is russet brown; later it becomes darker and split, furrowed with scaly ridges. The bark of *T. canadensis* has been widely used for tanning leather.

Mordant: Chrome gives a fine rose-tan.

Method: Break up the bark (especially the inner bark) and soak overnight in the water to be used for dyeing. Then heat the bath slowly and simmer for 1 to 1½ hours. Do not overboil or the color will be browned. Strain off the bark and cool the liquor. Add a pinch of alum if you wish to bring out an orange color. Enter the clean, wetted wool and return bath to the simmer. Simmer for 1½ hours. The rose-tan color of chromed wool can be enhanced by steeping in an afterbath of vinegar. Rinse the wool twice and dry.

3 LBS (1.5 KG) OR ABOUT 1 PK BARK, FRESH OR DRY

A PINCH OF ALUM (OPTIONAL)

AFTERBATH
3 TBSP VINEGAR PER GAL OF WATER

ANCHUSA OR ALKANET

Alkanna tinctoria or *Anchusa tinctoria* or *A. officinalis*

Various forms of anchusa (which is also known as alkanna, alcanea, and bugloss) grow wild in Europe and Britain, and garden forms have been developed for the fine blue of the flowers. It is an erect, very hairy stemmed plant that rises to 2 feet or more, with hairy single-pointed leaves swathing the stem. The flowers are like large, incredibly blue forget-me-nots, blooming usually in June. Pliny mentioned it as a dye plant, and Gerard's *Herbal* recommended it "drunke with hot beere," and said "The Gentlewomen of France do paint their faces with these roots."

Anchusa used to be cultivated as a dye plant in Europe, and early settlers in North America probably brought it over for medicinal use but maybe as a dye too. But the red it produces is rather fugitive, and the faster madder would be preferred where available. I grow it in my garden for its flowers. The roots have yielded me only a dull red hardly worth the trouble, so I use dried roots or an extract obtained from dye houses for dyeing.

Mordant: Alum gives a range from tan-red to purple-red and gray. An extra tablespoon of cream of tartar in the dyebath helps.

Method: Add the extract solution to the bath and heat until the extract is thoroughly dissolved or boil the roots for 2 hours and strain. Cool the liquor. Enter the clean, wetted wool and return bath to the simmer. Simmer for 20 to 40 minutes, according to the depth of color desired. Dry the wool without rinsing.

To preserve the blue color, enter the wool in an alkaline afterbath of ammonia for about a minute. To bring out the purple to red shades, dip the wool briefly in an acid bath. (Strengthen the ammonia solution if the water is very soft and the acetic acid if the water is hard.) Rinse the wool thoroughly and dry.

2 CUPS DRIED ROOTS

OR

½ OZ (15G) ALKANET EXTRACT DISSOLVED IN WATER OR ALCOHOL (I HAVE OBTAINED THE BEST PURPLE-REDS WITH ALCOHOL, BUT A LARGE QUANTITY OF WOOL WOULD REQUIRE TOO MUCH TO BE PRACTICAL)

AFTERBATH
2 TBSP AMMONIA

OR

3 TBSP ACETIC ACID PER ½ GAL OF WATER

IVY

Hedera helix

The familiar ivy is indigenous to Europe including Britain and to Asia, and is also now common in North America. The shining leather-like green leaves (sometimes variegated in cultivated kinds) with three to five lobes and the aerial roots that enable it to climb trees and walls make it easy to identify. The flowers, however, in small greenish yellow clusters, are far from obvious. Since not all kinds of ivy berry freely, many people are unaware what the fruit of the ivy is. I find that the loosely growing hedgerow type with scarcely lobed leaves yields most berries. In Europe the berries must be picked in February or March, when they are quite ripe and as black as possible — at any other time they give disappointing results. Gerard in his *Herbal* suggests gathering "after the Winter Solstice," and recommends an infusion for "waterish eies."

Mordant: None necessary, but alum may be used for yellow-green and iron added to the dyebath gives greenish gray.

Method: Steep the berries overnight in the water to be used for dyeing. Heat slowly and simmer for 1 hour. Strain off the berries and cool the liquor. Enter the clean, wetted wool and return bath to the simmer. Simmer for ½ hour. For a greenish gray, add iron to the bath and simmer for 10 to 30 minutes. Rinse the wool twice and dry.

6 OZ (180G) RIPE BERRIES

¼ TSP FERROUS SULFATE FOR GREENISH GRAY

Recipes For Summer

QUEEN OF THE MEADOW OR MEADOWSWEET

Filipendula ulmaria

This is a 3- to 6-foot-tall perennial that grows abundantly in damp and woods in both North Europe and Asia, and as a garden flower and as a wild escape in many parts of the United States. A frothy mass of creamy white flowers grows on top of reddish ribbed stems. The plant has up to five pairs of saw-edged leaflets on the lower leaves, and between these are distinctive pairs of little leaflets. Where the leaf springs from the stem are leafy stipules. Gerard, in his *Herbal* of 1597, said of queen of the meadow, "The leaves and floures farre excell all other strowing herbs, for to decke up houses; for the smell thereof meketh the heart merrie, delighteth the senses."

Meadowsweet roots were used in the Hebrides and other northern countries for black, but I get much better results from iris roots or alder bark. Winifred Shand, a Scottish rural specialist, also says the stalks and leaves give a navy blue, but I have not obtained it.

Mordant: Alum gives greenish yellow, iron added to the dyebath gives green.

Method: The simultaneous method of dying is preferable here. Put the tops in a mesh bag immediately after picking and enter together with the clean, wetted wool. Slowly bring bath to the simmer and simmer wool and flowers for ½ to 1 hour according to the depth of color desired.) Lift the bag out of the bath frequently and work the wool to keep the dyeing even. The color can be made more green by the addition of a few crystals of iron for the last 15 minutes. Rinse the wool twice and dry.

½ PK OR ABOUT ¾ PAIL TOPS JUST INTO FLOWER

A PINCH OF FERROUS SULFATE (FOR GREEN)

TANSY

Tanacetum vulgare

A 1- to 3-foot-high straight plant with ribbed stems, tansy is common on waste places and roadsides and is known by its distinctive scent like strong hot lemon. It used to be grown in cottage gardens for cooking and as a cure for colds. The fernlike leaves are covered with tiny glands, giving it a slightly gray appearance. The mustard-yellow flower heads are held in a cup of bracts and are apparently without petals, so they resemble a cluster of flat cushions. Tansy flowers later than ragwort (see page 46) and can be used as an alternative to it, though the color is not so strong. The plant can be dried, and keeps its scent.

Mordant: Alum gives yellow.

Method: If you cannot use the flower heads quite fresh, put them in the bath water until you are ready. Heat the bath slowly and simmer for ½ hour. Strain off the flower heads and cool the liquor. Enter the clean, wetted wool and return bath to the simmer. Simmer until the desired color is obtained. Rinse twice and dry. The color will be a stronger, less clear yellow if you have soaked the flowers beforehand.

½-1 LB (250G-5KG) OR ½ PK FULLY FLOWERING HEADS WITH BRACTS

HORSETAIL OR MARES' TAIL

Equisetum species

Horsetail is one of the most primitive plants still with us. A giant form of it must have existed over large land areas in the aeons before the more complex plants developed. The kind dyers use grows in ditches and waste places, especially where it is damp. It is easily recognizable: it resembles a miniature fir tree about 6 to 10 inches high, with rings of green "branches" springing in circles at decreasing intervals up the stem. The reproductive stalks, which carry long pollen caps on top and have paler stems, are not used in dyeing. The green stalks are cut off at ground level.

Mordant: Alum gives slightly yellowish green.

Method: Use very fresh plants. They can be simmered in the usual way, but with this plant, as with lichens, the contact method of dyeing is better. Put a layer of horsetails on the bottom of an enamel pan and cover with about a quarter of the wool. Then add another layer of horsetails, another layer of wool, and so on. Pour the water over all and heat slowly. Simmer together for up to ½ hour, but not too long, as this will dull the color. A brighter green can be obtained with an afterbath of copper sulfate at this point. Rinse the wool twice and dry.

Horsetails are said to be suitable for top-dyeing with blue but I have not tried it.

½-1 PK HORSETAIL PLANTS

AFTERBATH
1 TSP COPPER SULFATE PER GAL OF WATER

44

DAY LILY

Hemerocallis hybrids

This well-known perennial is grown mostly as a garden flower in Europe but now grows rampantly wild over parts of the United States. The many hybrids are derived from Japanese and Chinese species. They have long strap-like pointed leaves and a small cluster of lily-like flowers in orange, peach, or yellow shades, and grow about 2 to 4 feet high. They flower from June to September; each flower opens, blooms, and dies in one day, hence the name. They are best gathered towards the end of the day, when a pressed bloom will give a blue stain to paper. The buds are said to be a food delicacy.

Mordant: Alum gives yellow, tin gives bright yellow, copper sulfate gives blue-green with longer simmering.

Method: If you cannot use the flower heads at once, put them in a mesh bag in water and use this water as the dyebath. The simultaneous method is used. Enter the clean, wetted wool. Slowly bring bath to the simmer and simmer wool and flowers for 20 to 45 minutes, or longer if blue-green is required. In this case a few crystals of iron can be added for the last 15 minutes. Rinse the wool twice and dry.

1 TO 2 PT FLOWER HEADS PRESSED DOWN

A SMALL PINCH OF FERROUS SULFATE

WELD

Reseda luteola

Weld is known by a variety of names including dyer's rocket, dyer's weed, and wild mignonette. For many centuries it was used as a dye plant in Britain, being indigenous, but it was also cultivated; Rhind (in 1855) said the cultivated variety contained more coloring matter. It is still found wild, especially on the chalk Downs. It consists of 1½ - to 3-foot spike of tiny yellowish green flowers with deeply divided leaves. The wild plant is not scented like the garden mignonette but is a larger edition of similar form. Weld is perhaps the best of the British plants for dye fastness. It is very good for dyeing when dried, and can be gathered and hung up for winter use. It must be gathered before it seeds, for then it loses its coloring properties. Weld is also a good dye for silk, mordanted and treated in the same way as wool. A recipe for dyeing cotton is given on page 90.

Mordant: Alum with cream of tartar gives lemon yellow, chrome gives golden-yellow, tin gives bright orange-yellow, and iron added to the dyebath gives olive with alum-mordanted wool.

Method: Put the weld in cold water and heat slowly for 2 to 3 hours. Strain off the plant and cool the liquor. Enter the clean, wetted wool and return bath to the simmer. Simmer for about an hour according to the depth of color desired. For olive, add iron for the last 15 minutes. Rinse the wool twice and dry.

In the traditional industry, a little lime was added to the brew, but I have not tried it.

½ PK OR ½-¾ PAIL CHOPPED UP WHOLE PLANTS, PREFERABLY PICKED JUST BEFORE THEY FLOWER

½ TSP FERROUS SULFATE (FOR OLIVE)

YELLOW FLAG IRIS

Iris pseudacorus

This handsome plant, whose name came from the Greek *i-ris,* meaning rainbow, can grow up to 6 feet high, but is more commonly 3 feet high. It is found wild in Britain and as an escape in parts of the United States in ponds, slow rivers, and marshes. Its long, swordlike leaves and head of three up-curving bearded plumes and three down-bending banners or "falls" are unmistakable. Although bisexual, the flower cannot pollinate itself. I have not been able to obtain a color from many garden varieties, nor from the blue iris *sibirica.* The black dye from the yellow flag iris was until recently used in the Hebrides for the black garments frequently worn by the women of the islands.

Mordant: Iron gives black.

Method: I have experimented with using the brown outer covering of the root, the small rootlets, and the rhizomes alone, but have not found much difference, so I just use the whole root, which I cut up with strong scissors. Put the roots in cold water and heat slowly. Simmer for 1 to 2 hours. Strain off the roots and cool the liquor. Enter the clean, wetted wool and return to the simmer. A gray color is obtained quickly, a real black after 2 to 3 hours. Rinse the wool twice and dry.

1-2 LBS (.5-1 KG) OR 2-4 QTS ROOTS, CHOPPED UP

RAGWORT OR TANSY RAGWORT

Senecio jacobaea

A tall weed of waste places and neglected fields, also called ragweed (but not to be confused with the ragweed, hogweed, or bitterweed of the United States), this is common over Europe and is somewhat of an escape in eastern North America. The stiff upright stems, growing to 2 or 2½ feet, carry much-divided curving leaves and clusters of small yellow daisy-like heads, with a ragged corolla of strong yellow. The plant has a strong, rather unpleasant smell and is redolent of high summer. There are 1,200 species of *Senecio* around the world and many of them probably yield a dye but the others I have tried are not so strong.

Mordant: Alum gives strong yellow, iron added to the dyebath gives green.

Method: The heads are best for yellow, but the whole upper part of the plant may be used for green. Put the plant in cold water and heat slowly. Simmer for ½ hour. Strain off the plant and cool the liquor.

For yellow, enter the clean, wetted wool and return bath to the simmer only until the wool has absorbed the color. Prolonged simmering will brown the color. For green, enter the wool and return bath to the simmer. Simmer until a good depth of color has been obtained. Add the iron for the last 15 minutes. Too much iron or prolonged boiling will gray the color. Rinse the wool twice and dry.

1 QT FLOWER HEADS OR 1 PK WHOLE UPPER PART OF PLANT

SCANT ½ TSP FERROUS SULFATE (FOR GREEN)

ST.-JOHN'S WORT

Hypericum species

St.-John's-wort is a wild flower of the pastures and waysides over Europe and much of North America. Several cultivated varieties give dye. The stems are clothed with opposite pairs of lanceolate leaves, lighter below and capped with five yellow shining flowers that open from a red-tinged bud to a cupped head in July and August. But this plant has one quite distinctive feature to identify. If you hold the leaves up to the light, you can see that the tissue is almost perforated by pin-point holes; hence the old name *perforata*. Traditionally, the flower heads were used to obtain a red dye, which Violetta Thurston (who recorded plant dyes in England many years ago) says can be extracted with acetic acid. As I have not been very successful with this color, I give the recipe for yellow, for which the whole of the tops can be used. They do not need to be flowering.

Mordant: Alum gives clear medium yellow, chrome gives strong buttercup yellow.

Method: I find that the tips of the sprays in early summer before the flowers appear give a very good dye but the plant can be used right through until autumn with the flower heads on. The simultaneous method is preferable. Put the tips in a mesh bag and enter together with the clean, wetted wool. Slowly bring bath to the simmer and simmer wool and plant for ½ hour or until a strong clear color is obtained. Lift the bag out of the bath frequently and work the wool to keep the dyeing even. Rinse the wool twice and dry.

1 QT (PACKED) TIPS: THEY DO NOT NEED TO BE FLOWERING

DAHLIA

Dahlia species

The familiar dahlias of flower gardens have an extraordinarily strong dye (for flowers) in their petals. The color varies with the color of the petals, from yellow to orange-red. I have dyed an ounce of wool with one large dahlia head ready to be thrown out after a week in a vase, so the flowers serve a double purpose and one is spared the rather painful task of ripping off heads in full flower for dye. The dye is very fast when used on chrome-mordanted wool. The common red geranium (*Pelargonium* species) gives a similar range of color by the same recipe.

Mordant: Alum gives yellow to bronze-gold, chrome gives tan to orange-red.

Method: Put flower heads in cold water and heat slowly. Simmer for 12 to 15 minutes. Strain off the heads and cool the liquor. Enter the clean, wetted wool and return bath to the simmer. Simmer for 12 to 20 minutes for yellows, longer for bronze or red. Rinse the wool twice and dry.
The simultaneous method of dyeing can also be used.

10-30 FLOWER HEADS, DEPENDING ON SIZE

½ LB (250G) OR ½ PK FLOWERING TOPS, INCLUDING SMALL LEAVES AND STEMS, CUT UP LIGHTLY

½ LB (250G) OR ½ PK FRESH FLOWER HEADS, OR DOUBLE THIS QUANTITY OF STEMS AND LEAVES, BROKEN UP

---

1 TSP FERROUS SULFATE (FOR YELLOW-GREEN)

AFTERBATH (FOR TAN-YELLOW)
A PINCH OF CHROME
AND
A FEW DROPS ACETIC ACID PER GAL OF WATER

DYER'S GREENWOOD

Genista tinctoria

Dyer's broom, dyer's weed, woodwaxen, woad-waxen, and greenweed are some of the names by which this plant is known. (It is not to be confused with weld, which is also called dyer's weed.) The names greenwood and woad-waxen refer to old custom of using it over indigo or woad to make green. A 4- to 5-foot shrub, it is found in Europe and Asia, and grows wild on sandy soil on the temperate east coast of America. Before it became naturalized in the United States, it was imported ground, in casks. Brought to the new world for dye purposes, the plant escaped to grow wild there. In Salem, Massachusetts, site of the famous New England witch trials, it was called "witches blood" because it bloomed on Gallows Hill. It is still common in those parts. It is recognizably of the broom family but has very small single leaves springing, almost without stem, from the light branches. The flower is yellow and pealike, and continues to flower all summer if pruned back well. It needs sun to thrive. It is one of the surest, most firm yellow vegetable dyes.

Mordant: Alum gives clear light yellow, chrome gives warm yellow.

Method: Put the tops in cold water and heat slowly. Simmer for 1 hour. Strain off the tops and cool the liquor. Enter the clean, wetted wool and return bath to the simmer. Simmer for up to 1 hour, according to the depth of color desired. Rinse the wool twice and dry.

GOLDENROD

Solidago species, especially *S. canadensis*

Goldenrod is a 2- to 5-foot perennial with tiny yellow daisy-like florets frothed into flower heads. It grows wild in many parts of North America and Europe and is grown in country gardens of both continents. It has a hot strong smell. The flower heads, cut or broken off with some stem, are used when they are just coming into flower, and some part of the plant — sprays lower down the stem — can be found flowering over most of the summer. The flowers can be dried in the shade for future use, but are better fresh. Any part of the plant will give a dye, but the yellow color is best from the sprays of flower heads.

Mordant: Alum gives clear lemon yellow to tan-yellow, chrome gives warm old gold. Iron added to the dyebath with stems and leaves gives yellow-green.

Method: If you cannot use the flower heads quite fresh, put them in the bath water until you are ready. Heat the bath slowly and simmer for ½ to 1 hour. Strain off the plant and cool the liquor. Enter the clean, wetted wool and return bath to the simmer. Simmer for 10 to 20 minutes or more according to the depth of color desired. To obtain green, add iron when a strong color has been obtained and simmer 15 minutes more. To obtain a deep tan-yellow with alum-mordanted wool, enter it in a chrome afterbath and simmer covered for 15 to 45 minutes according to the depth of color desired. Rinse the wool twice and dry (away from the light if you have used chrome).

The simultaneous method of dyeing can also be used.

PRICKLY-PEAR CACTUS

Opuntia polycantha

There are some 300 *Opuntia* species native to North and South America but I have tried only this. This species, with fat pear-shaped fruits sprouting from flattish gray-green pads with thin spiny prickles, grows around the Mediterranean (where people carefully peel the prickled outer skin of the fruit to savor the soft flesh within) and in New Mexico, Arizona, and other southern states. It is easily propagated by sticking a cut "pad," or joint, in sandy soil.

Mordant: None necessary.

Method: The American Indians are said to rub the fruits in the sand with their feet to remove the prickles — I peel them with leather gloves on. Mash or pound the fruit in a bucket and add the water. The bucket should be plastic or pottery, not metal. Enter the clean, wetted wool and leave the whole *in a warm place* for 10 days or longer to ferment. Work the wool from time to time. Rinse the wool and dry. If, after rinsing, a deeper color is required, repeat the process: put the dyed wool in a new bath of fresh fruit and leave for another 10 days or longer. No simmering is involved as this causes the reds and pinks to go tan.

1 LB (.5KG) OR 1½ PKS FRESH CACTUS FRUITS

MARIGOLD

Tagetes species

These marigolds are different from the marsh marigold (*Caltha palustris*), which also makes a dye. They are yellow to orange flowers common in Britain, and indigenous to the southwestern United States, Mexico, and South America. They have been developed into many varieties of garden flower. Marigolds are annuals, and they flower so freely that I do not mind using some from my garden for dye. However, cold winters tend to kill the seed. The lower leaves are stalked, the upper ones clasp the stem. The conspicuous flower heads with yellow corolla are the source of the dye. (The marigold should not be confused with yellow camomile, which also makes a dye — camomile is smaller and has deeply divided leaves.) Silk can be dyed in the same way as wool. A recipe for dyeing cotton is given on page 91.

Mordant: Alum gives yellow, chrome gives warm golden yellow.

Method: Put the heads in cold water and heat slowly. Simmer for ¾ hour. Strain off the heads and cool the liquor. Enter the clean, wetted wool and return bath to the simmer. Simmer for ¾ to 1 hour. Keep covered if you are using chrome-mordanted wool. Rinse the wool twice and dry.

The simultaneous method of dyeing may also be used.

1 LB (.5KG) OR ½ PK FRESH FLOWER HEADS. IF DRIED FLOWER HEADS ARE USED, REDUCE THE QUANTITY SLIGHTLY

COREOPSIS OR CALLIOPSIS
Coreopsis tinctoria also known as *C. marmorata*

Coreopsis (from the Greek meaning "buglike") is also called tickseed. *C. tinctoria* is one of 70 species of coreopsis native to America, where it is found both wild and cultivated. In Britain it is usually a garden plant, which is annual but seeds itself freely; others are perennial, single or double. The rather glabrous 1- to 3-foot-high plant has leaves deeply divided into linear lobes, and heads ¾ to 3 inches across. It flowers from July to October. Many colors of garden varieties, from yellow through crimson to maroon, have been bred from the original, which has a center disc and ray of petals.

Mordant: Chrome gives burnt orange, tin gives bright yellow.

Method: The simultaneous method of dyeing is preferable here. Put the flower heads in a mesh bag and enter together with the clean, wetted wool. Soft water is especially important for coreopsis. Slowly bring bath to the simmer and simmer wool and flower heads for 20 minutes or longer, according to the depth of color desired. Lift the bag out of the bath frequently and work the wool to keep the dyeing even. Rinse the wool twice and dry.
Wool freshly mordanted with tin and cream of tartar is best but I have used wool formerly mordanted and just added a pinch of cream of tartar to the simmering bath. In any case, with tin and cream of tartar rinse in soapy water first, then in clear water, and dry.

½ PK FLOWER HEADS

BROOM
Cytisus, Genista, and *Spartium* species

Genista gave its name to the Plantagenet kings, and a sprig of this broom is worn by the young Richard II in the lovely Wilton diptych in the National Gallery, London. Hardy in the central United States and Europe, the *Spartium* species is distinguished from the others by its height — up to 10 feet — its sparsely leaved branches, and its one-lipped calyx. *Cytisus,* which needs a mild climate, has a wider range of flower colors, including even purple. Of the three, the traditional *Genista tinctoria* is much the best dye plant, but most of the varieties commonly called broom that have a yellow, pealike flower will give a yellow dye from the flowering tips. The flowering tips with the green stems will give a greenish yellow. For a pure yellow, use the flower heads alone. In Scotland broom has long been used over indigo for a good green.

Mordant: Alum gives yellow, chrome gives deep yellow.

Method: If you cannot use the tips quite fresh, put them in the bath water until you are ready. Heat the bath slowly and simmer for up to 1 hour. As the tips are a fragile part of the plant, however, the freshest color will be obtained by using the simultaneous method of dyeing.

1½ LBS (.75KG) OR 1 PK BRANCH TIPS, CHOPPED

Recipes For Autumn

CYPRESS

Chamaecyparis species especially *C. lawsoniana*

These pointed, feathery evergreens have long been associated with church-yards, and their distinctive dark cone-shape patterns the landscape. One of the commonest species, *lawsoniana,* is a native of the Pacific coast of the United States but is hardy in colder regions. It is tall with flat, spreading fronds, in contrast to the erect fronds of the bluish, glabrous species, which may also yield dyes. Gather the pale tan-orange cones before they fall from the trees.

Mordant: Alum or chrome gives bright tan.

Method: The simultaneous method of dyeing is preferable here. Put the cones in a mesh bag and enter together with the clean, wetted wool. Slowly bring bath to the simmer and simmer wool and cones for 40 minutes or longer. Lift the bag out of the bath frequently and work the wool to keep the dyeing even. To sharpen the color, you can add tin for the last 15 minutes. To dull the color, use iron instead in the same way. Rinse the wool twice and dry.

1 QT OR MORE RIPE CONES

¼ TSP STANNOUS CHLORIDE
OR
¼ TSP FERROUS SULFATE (OPTIONAL)

1-2 QTS BARK

AFTERBATH
SCANT ⅛ TSP FERROUS SULFATE
AND
2 TBSP VINEGAR PER GAL OF WATER

BLACK WILLOW

Salix nigra

The black willow is native to North America but is also found in Europe and Britain. It has long, pendulous branches, downy twigs, and toothed leaves that are dark green above and almost bluish underneath. The male and female catkins grow on different trees. I find that black willow gives a rosier color than white willow, which is much more common in Britain and Europe.

Mordant: Alum gives rosy tan, chrome gives warm brown.

Method: Soak the bark overnight in the water to be used for dyeing. Then heat the bath slowly and simmer for 2 hours. Strain off the bark and cool the liquor. Enter the clean, wetted wool and return bath to the simmer. Simmer for ½ hour. Without rinsing, enter the wool immediately in the afterbath, which should be simmering. Simmer for 10 minutes. Rinse the wool twice and dry.

WILD GRAPE VINE

Vitis species

3-4 QTS GRAPES, CRUSHED

AFTERBATH (FOR PURPLE)
3 TBSP ACETIC ACID PER ½ GAL OF WATER

The wild vine that I found in the mountains of Pennsylvania is only one of many grape species common to different parts of the United States, where delicious wine is produced from some kinds. The leaves of the wild vine I found are smaller and the grapes very much smaller than those of the cultivated Old World types, but with its tendrils the plant climbs up out of the hillside undergrowth into the sunlight.

It is interesting to note that the French vineyards were almost destroyed by the grape root louse until it was found that native American species were immune to the pest. Now most Old World grapes are grafted on cuttings or young plants of American stock in areas where the root louse is prevalent.

Mordant: Alum gives lavender to purplish gray, chrome gives reddish purple.

Method: The berries crushed make a fairly effective stain, but in order to get the color thoroughly absorbed into the wool, it is necessary to simmer it. The simultaneous method is best. Put the grapes in a mesh bag and enter together with the clean, wetted wool. Slowly bring bath to the simmer and simmer wool and grapes for 15 to 30 minutes. Lift the bag out of the bath frequently and work the wool to keep the dyeing even. To bring out the purple, enter the wool in a warm acid afterbath for about 10 minutes. Simmering is not necessary here. I find it quite effective to dry the wool slowly before steeping and then rinse it thoroughly in warm water and dry again.

BLACK CURRANT

Ribes nigrum

The common garden black currant, too well known to merit description, gives a number of pleasant colors. I put an open pan or cooking dish of the freshly gathered currants in a very low oven to draw out the juice, which contains the dye, and strain off the berries, which lose some of their flavor but can still be used combined with other fruit in pies or other dishes. In winter I use the liquid from bottled or canned currants. The colors are beautiful but not very fast.

Mordant: Alum gives deep lilac, tin gives purple.

Method: The simultaneous method of dyeing is preferable here. Put the wool in the bath and slowly bring it to the simmer. Simmer wool and juice for ½ to 1 hour. As the syrupy juice is apt to stick to the pan, be sure to work the wool frequently. Make the bath up to 2/3 gallon (not the usual full gallon) with additional water if it boils away. Leave the wool soaking in the bath for several hours. By then alum-mordanted wool will be a deep heather pink, which rinses out to strong lilac. Tin-mordanted wool will be a deep purple which rinses out (use soapy water) to a soft purple. Dry.

1/3 GAL BLACK CURRANT JUICE OR CRUSHED BLACK CURRANTS MADE UP TO 2/3 GAL WITH WATER

LARCH

Larix species

Larch, one of the deciduous members of the pine family, yields a useful if not very exciting dye for those who need to gather dye material to use indoors in winter. It has a dark, furrowed, scaly bark (redder in the Japanese larch). The leaves, very bright yellow-green in spring, are arranged spirally in clusters on short spurs. The bright green cones (bluish in the Japanese form) are ¾ to 1½ inches long. The soft needles can be gathered when green and stored, or can be picked up where they fall in piles in autumn.

Mordant: Alum gives brown.

Method: Put the needles in cold water and heat slowly. Simmer for 1½ hours. Strain off the needles and cool the liquor. Enter the clean, wetted wool and return bath to the simmer. Simmer until the desired depth of color is obtained. Rinse the wool twice and dry.

1 LB (.5KG) OR ½ PK NEEDLES

NORWAY MAPLE

Acer platanoides

This large tree with a head that spreads a hundred feet is common in the temperate zones of Europe. It is related to the native maples of the eastern United States. I have tried some of these, which gave a similar dye. The leaves are 3 to 5 inches long, with five pointed lobes, and the fruits have two spreading wings for seed dispersal. When young, the leaves are reddish in color. I have heard that country people in America used rotted maple wood with ferrous sulfate to make a purple dye, but I have not been able to obtain this. All barks, having tannin, tend to produce a brown color, but the Norway maple dye has an interesting pinkish tinge. The bark should be taken from a felled tree, and may be used either fresh or dried. It would also be worthwhile to experiment with other maples.

Mordant: Chrome gives pinkish tan.

Method: Enter the bark in cold water and heat slowly. Simmer for about 1½ hours. Strain off the bark and cool the liquor. Enter the clean, wetted wool and return bath to the simmer. Simmer for about 1 hour. The color will be improved by steeping the wool in a warm afterbath of copper sulfate for about 20 minutes. Rinse twice and dry.

½ PK STRIPPED BARK

AFTERBATH
1½ TSP COPPER SULFATE PER GAL OF WATER

LOMBARDY POPLAR

Populus nigra italica

This very narrow tall poplar tree is planted in avenues especially in Italy, and its heart-shaped leaves quiver in the wind. A native of Central Asia, the tree was brought from Italy to England by an ambassador in the mid-eighteenth century and has spread widely. I always used the leaves green for dyeing until I found, quite by accident, that dried leaves also work, when the tree in my garden was cut down by a workman, and only withered branches were left. The dried leaves give an unusual color. If you use dried leaves, be sure to remove all the twigs, as the tannin in them will dull the color.

Mordant: Alum gives soft yellow and chrome a golden yellow if green leaves are used; dried leaves give a duller khaki yellow.

Method: If possible, steep the leaves overnight in the water to be used for dyeing. Slowly heat the bath and simmer for 1 hour. Strain off the leaves and cool the liquor. Enter the clean, wetted wool and return bath to the simmer. Simmer for 1 to 2 hours. Rinse the wool twice and dry.

1 LB (.5KG) OR 1 PK GREEN LEAVES OR
HALF THIS AMOUNT OF DRIED LEAVES

PYRACANTHA OR FIRETHORN

Pyracantha angustifolia

This shrub (which used to be classed with cotoneasters) originated in China but is now very common in gardens and parks. The rigid purplish brown branches bear fierce thorns, and the lanceolate leaves with minutely serrated edges are dark green above and gray-felted below. The clusters of white flowers that the tree bears in June develop into orange or red berries that make it very decorative. The tree must be pruned back because of its thorns, so I use the clippings for dye. The bark can be easily stripped from the stems if one wears gloves. *P. coccinea* is a hardier species, more popular in the U.S., but I have not tried it.

Mordant: Alum gives yellow, chrome gives pinkish brown.

Method: If possible, steep the bark overnight in the water to be used for dyeing. Slowly heat the bath and simmer for 1 to 2 hours. Strain off the bark and cool the liquor. Enter the clean, wetted wool and return bath to the simmer for up to 2 hours. To warm the color, enter the wool in a chrome afterbath; to brighten it, use a tin afterbath, and to dull it to a gray-green, use iron. In all cases the afterbath should be simmering when the wool is entered. Simmer the wool for 10 minutes, not longer, to avoid the side effects of these chemicals. Rinse the wool twice and dry.

1 QT (PACKED) BARK

AFTERBATH
1 TSP CHROME
OR
SCANT 1 TSP FERROUS SULFATE
OR
SCANT 1 TSP STANNOUS CHLORIDE PER GAL
OF WATER

SLOE OR BLACKTHORN

Prunus spinosa

This spiny, black-twigged form of plum, native to Eurasia, is now found all over Europe, as an escape in North America, and in parts of Asia. A frail powdering of delicate small white flowers often clothes the bushes before the leaves appear and makes splashes of white in the prickly hedges. The leaves are lanceolate and toothed. In autumn the small hard blue-black fruits appear; although rounder, they resemble tiny plums, with the characteristic groove. Sloe gin is a traditional country restorative and is still made by enthusiasts, among whom I number myself. The bark also gives a dye, a red-brown color. Sloe dyes silk even better than wool.

Mordant: None necessary for a rose-pink, but alum improves the fastness of the color.

Method: The simultaneous method of dyeing is preferable here. Put the sloes in a mesh bag and enter in the bath together with the clean, wetted wool. Slowly bring bath to the simmer and simmer berries and wool for about 40 minutes. Lift the bag out of the bath frequently and work the wool to keep the dyeing even. Rinse the wool twice and dry. If the wool is washed in soapy water before rinsing, the color will turn grayish blue because soap is alkaline.

½ LB (250G) OR ABOUT 1 QT BERRIES, FRESHLY PICKED AND WELL BRUISED. IT IS NOT ABSOLUTELY NECESSARY TO REMOVE THE STONES.

7

Facing page: A student's first weaving, done on a rough frame loom. The fiber was dyed with birch and cherry, and the barks of birch and cherry have been incorporated in the weaving.

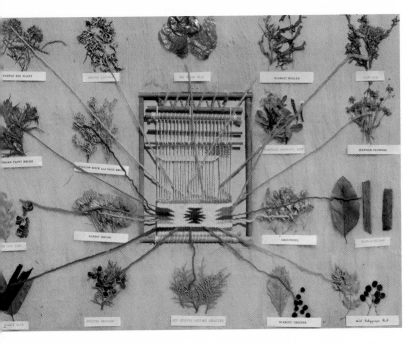

8

Left: American Indian dye-plants and a weaving made with fibers dyed by these plants. (Photograph courtesy of Jacqueline Enthoven)

9,10

Below and below left: Two weavings by students of the author. The fibers of the piece at left were dyed with barks; the other piece was dyed with onion skins and weld.

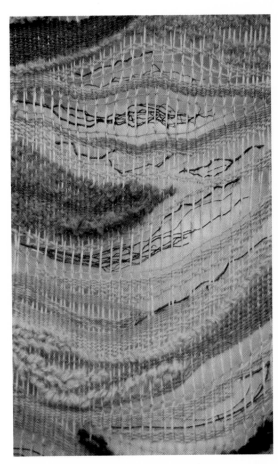

POKEWEED OR POKEBERRY

Phytolacca americana

Also called scoke, pigeon berry, pokan, coakum, inkberry, redweed, bear's grape, garget, and other names, this 3- to 10-foot-tall glabrous plant springs from a large, poisonous root, which is perennial. The leaves are 5 to 12 inches long. The white flowers grow in terminal racemes, each floret composed of 4 to 5 narrow petals. These develop into dark purple ten-ribbed berries, which are a favorite food of birds but poisonous to humans. Pokeweed grows from Ontario in Canada east to Maine and south to Arkansas, Florida, and Mexico. It has been naturalized in many parts of Europe. The plant is a troublesome weed, so dyers will be thanked for removing its berries before it seeds. However, when the first shoots are very young they can be eaten like asparagus and are delicious. According to Bryant *(Navajo Indian Dyes),* the Navajo Indians used the root bark of poke weed along with that of plum for purple-brown, and I am told that the reddish-tinged leaves and the stems will make a dye, but I have used only the berries, which give interesting but not very fast colors.

Mordant: Alum gives reds to soft tan.

Method: Since simmering the berries too long will result in a brown rather than a pink to rose color, I steep them overnight and then use the simultaneous method. Put the berries in a mesh bag and enter in the bath together with the clean, wetted wool. Bring bath to the simmer and simmer wool and berries for ½ hour or longer. Lift the bag out of the bath frequently and work the wool to keep the dyeing even. Leave the wool to cool in the bath for several hours. Fine pinks from flesh to rose are obtained from a shorter simmering. Rinse the wool twice and dry.

At the Penland School of Handicrafts the berries are simmered in a strong vinegar-water mixture instead of using water alone. This should deepen the pink color. If the wool is washed in soapy water before rinsing, it turns grayish blue.

¾-1½ LBS (360 G-.75 KG) OR ½ QT VERY RIPE BERRIES, CRUSHED

BLACK HUCKLEBERRY

Gaylussacia baccata

This well-known shrub grows only 1 to 3 feet high but spreads horizontally with broad lanceolate blunt leaves about an inch long. The white or pink to reddish flowers only a quarter of an inch across in a bell-like corolla, grow in loose pointed clusters. The plant prefers sandy or rocky acid soil but is also found in swampy moors. It grows from Newfoundland to Florida, and its familiar black berry is well known in American and Canadian kitchens. I have used dried and even canned huckleberries as well as fresh berries. The colors are beautiful but not very fast. I use huckleberry for embroidery threads, where the washing qualities are not important.

Mordant: Alum or chrome for shades of purple.

Method: Steep dry berries overnight in the water to be used for dyeing; crush fresh berries lightly. (You can use half the quantities if you wish.) The simultaneous method of dyeing is used. Put the berries in a mesh bag and enter in the bath, along with any juices, together with the clean, wetted wool. Slowly bring the bath to the simmer and simmer wool and berries for ½ to 1 hour. Lift the bag out of the bath frequently and work the wool to keep the dyeing even. Allow the wool to cool in the bath. Rinse twice and dry.

2 LBS (1 KG) OR 1 QT BERRIES, FRESH OR CANNED; HALF THIS AMOUNT OF DRIED BERRIES

BIG-BUD HICKORY

Carya tomentosa

This well-known eastern North American tree, also called mocker nut, has a puckered bark and seven to nine pinnate-toothed leaves, which are fragrant when crushed. The light brown pear- or egg-shaped nut has a thick stalk and a sweet kernel. When no fruits are to be seen, the tree can be distinguished by its ridged bark and hairy twigs. Like other members of the species, it has long, drooping male catkins.

Hickory bark has long been known as a dye. In the eighteenth century a patent was taken out for it, but this was not very productive, since brighter yellows were available. The color fastness is good. Hickory twigs and leaves give a tan color with cream of tartar and Glauber's salts. Shellbark hickory also gives a dye from the green hulls.

Mordant: Alum gives yellow.

Method: Put the bark in cold water and heat slowly. Simmer for 3 hours. Strain off the bark and cool the liquor. Enter the clean, wetted wool and return bath to the simmer. Simmer for 1 to 3 hours. Rinse the wool twice and dry.

4 OZ (120 G) OR A BIG HANDFUL OF BARK, CRUSHED OR POUNDED WITH A HAMMER.

SUMAC OR SUMACH

Rhus species

This family is native to temperate and subtropical regions of both Americas, of Asia, and of Europe. The Arabs, in their conquest of Sicily, brought the "dyers sumac," *R, coriaria*, to Europe. Rhind speaks of this as giving a non-mordant yellow-green dye and mentions also that the seeds were used as an appetizer before meals. The leaves are also used for tanning leather. I have usually dyed a drab tan from the bright red berries of staghorn sumac (*R. typhina*), but in Pennsylvania in October, when glowing with red all through, they yielded a warm red. I have read that the Navajos make a warm orange from the fermented berries of *R. trilobata.* Traditionally, several ancient writers tell us, the shoots of sumac trees were cut down each year, and used for yellow dye. They give a stronger dye if dried and cut up. I have obtained a yellow from young leaves.

Sumac also dyes cotton, and a recipe is given on page 92. Care should be taken that one does not experiment with any of the poisonous sumacs. *R. radicans* (poison ivy) and *R. vernix* (swamp sumac, found only in boggy ground) are the two main culprits. Foliage of both colors beautifully in autumn, and both have *white* berries when ripe. There are several other American and Asian species which are also poisonous to touch.

Mordant: Alum gives brown, chrome gives warm tan.

Method: Put the berries in cold water and steep overnight in the water to be used for dyeing. Heat slowly and simmer for 2 hours or more. Strain off the berries and cool the liquor. Enter the clean, wetted wool and return bath to the simmer. Test the color after 20 minutes and remove the wool from the bath if it is a good tan as further simmering will dull the color. Rinse the wool twice and dry.

2 LBS (1 KG) OR ½ PK VERY RIPE BERRIES, BRUISED.

Recipes For Winter

HEATHER

Erica species, especially ling (*E. calluna vulgaris)* and some *E. carnea*

Heaths and heathers, low plants of heaths and moors, are very common over Europe, especially Scandinavia, and in Asia Minor. They are not wild or native in North America, but may be found in gardens. All the heathers yield a yellow dye, but that from ling is probably the best and has been used in Scotland and Ireland for centuries. Heather grows only in acid soil especially on peat, which is still used for fuel in these countries and in Scandinavia. Its pinkish (and occasionally white or red) flowers are tiny bells that create miles of distinctive purply-pink landscape when it blooms in late summer. Heather is perhaps best used when it is fresh and green, but it can be cut while it is green and dried for winter use.

Mordant: Alum gives yellow.

Method: Put the tips in cold water and heat slowly. Simmer for ½ to 1 hour (some dyers say 3 to 4 hours). Strain off the tips and cool the liquor. Enter the clean, wetted wool and return bath to the simmer. Simmer for about 1 hour, according to the depth of color desired. (Violetta Thurston says the addition of oak galls towards the end of dyeing will give a moss green.) Rinse the wool twice and dry.

½ LB (250G) OR 2-4 QTS FRESH OR DRIED TIPS

ALDER

Black Alder — *Alnus glutinosa*
Mountain Alder — *A. tenuifolia*

The alders are deciduous trees related to the birch family, but with woody cones, that grow in almost every part of Europe and much of North America but prefer the damper, temperate regions. The male catkins are swinging tails of yellow pollen; the female catkins are dark brown and remain dry on the tree after their fertilized scales have been released. The Navajo Indians use the male mountain alder, which has falling catkins of fine bracts, for dye. The leaves of the alder will produce a yellow dye, but since there are so many yellows, the bark is a more interesting dye material. It can be used fresh or dried.

Mordant: Alum gives yellowish brown. Add iron and copper sulfate to the dyebath for black.

Method: Steep the bark overnight in the water to be used for dyeing; if the bark is dried, steep it for a few days. Heat slowly and simmer for 2 hours. Strain off the bark and cool the liquor. Enter the clean, wetted wool and return bath to the simmer for 1 hour for a middle brown, 2 or more hours for a darker brown. To obtain warm black, add the iron and copper sulfate, simmer for 1½ hours more, and leave to cool in the bath. Rinse the wool twice and dry.

½ LB (250G) OR 1 PK FRESH OR DRIED BARK, PREFERABLY GATHERED IN MAY

1 TSP FERROUS SULFATE
AND
½ TSP COPPER SULFATE (FOR BLACK)

61

½ PK BARK

AFTERBATH
SCANT ½ TSP CHROME
AND
2 TBSP VINEGAR PER GAL OF WATER

CHERRY

Prunus species, especially European bird cherry *(P. padus)*

All the cherries I have tried yield a dye more or less interesting, but the bird cherry gives a warm pinkish color that becomes almost chocolate with long boiling as the brown of the tannin is extracted. This species grows in Europe and Asia. The leaves are shining green above, with a broadly tapering base. They are finely toothed and the leaf stalk has glands. The small white flowers hang from leafy stalks in drooping racemes. The fruit is small, round, and black. There are numerous native American cherries, all worth trying. Sloe (see page 55) and plum are related dye plants. The recipe for plum is the same as for cherry.

Mordant: Alum gives yellow to chocolate brown.

Method: Steep the bark overnight in the water to be used for dyeing. Heat slowly and simmer for about 2 hours. Strain off the bark and cool the liquor. Enter the clean, wetted wool and return bath to the simmer. Simmer for ½ to 3 hours. Immediately enter the wool in a simmering afterbath of chrome and vinegar. Simmer, covered, for 10 minutes. Rinse twice and dry.

MOUNTAIN LAUREL OR CALICO BUSH

Kalmia latifolia

1 LB (.5KG) OR 1-2 PKS LEAVES

½ TSP FERROUS SULFATE (FOR GRAY-BROWN)

This very common evergreen shrub of temperate America is grown in gardens in Britain and Europe. Few native American shrubs are more decorative. It is a rhododendron-like bush with large, oval, deep green glossy leaves and showy pale pink clusters of umbrella-like flowers. It likes acid soil and grows in both sun and shade. The leaves are used fresh, though they will also yield dye when dried. As the plant is evergreen, there are always green leaves to use, but the color obtained varies according to the season.

Mordant: Chrome gives soft to deep yellow, iron gives gray, and chrome with iron added to the dyebath gives gray-browns.

Method: Put the leaves in cold water and heat slowly. Simmer for 1 hour. Strain off the leaves and cool the liquor. Enter the clean, wetted wool and return bath to the simmer. Simmer for 1 hour. For gray or gray-brown (if chrome-mordanted wool has been used), add the iron for about the last 15 minutes of dyeing. Rinse the wool twice and dry.

SNOWBERRY OR WAXBERRY

Symphoricarpos albus

This 3- or 4-foot-high deciduous shrub is native to North America as far south as Mexico and as far north as Alaska. In Britain it is a common garden shrub and there are many wild escapes. The slender waving branches have opposite pairs of round-oval leaves. In July and August the reddish brown stems terminate in small clusters of tiny pink bell-like flowers, which produce the distinctive white berries that hang on through winter. This is one of the dyestuffs that can be gathered even with snow on the ground. The 6-foot-high variety *laevigatus* is recommended for gardens because the fruit clusters are larger, but I have not tried it for dyeing.

Mordant: Alum gives many shades of yellow from brilliant acid yellow through lime yellow to primrose yellow.

Method: Put the berries in cold water and heat slowly. Simmer for 1 hour. For the brilliant shades, leave the berries in the liquor and cool. Enter the clean, wetted wool and return bath to the simmer for ½ to 1 hour. Then leave the wool to steep in the bath for 1 to 3 days, stirring occasionally. If on the other hand you want the softer yellows, strain off the berries before cooling and entering the wool. Return bath to the simmer and simmer for ½ to 1 hour. For a khaki yellow, steep the berries for 24 hours before dyeing, simmer them for 1 hour, strain, cool, and simmer the wool for 1 hour. Rinse the wool twice and dry. There are probably many variations of this dye still to be explored.

2 LBS (1 KG) OR MORE FULLY WHITE BERRIES, LIGHTLY CRUSHED

BARBERRY

Berberis vulgaris

This prickly shrub with arching branches is native to Europe and eastern Asia and is naturalized in the eastern part of North America. It was apparently one of the first fruits sent over the New World in the early colonial days, for medicinal use as well as for eating. It used to grow wild in England, but the belief (called by Rhind a "vulgar prejudice") that it affected the growth of corn caused it to be banished from the hedgerows. Thus it is now more familiar to the British as a decorative garden shrub, grown for its flaming autumn foliage and flattish red berries, which used to be made into jelly and comfits with an acid flavor. Barberry has long been used as a yellow dye among European peasants.

Norwegian sources specially mention the use of the tips, and the whole plant is used in Greece, but I prefer the bark and roots. When the bush needs pruning I use the trimmings, which give rather less color. Any part can be dried for future use.

Barberry is a good dye for silk.

Mordant: None necessary. Alum gives light bright yellow, tin gives stronger yellows.

Method: Put the bark in cold water and heat slowly. Simmer for 1 to 2 hours. Strain off the bark and cool the liquor. Enter the clean, wetted wool and return bath to the simmer. Simmer for 1 hour. A stronger color can be obtained by leaving the wool in the bath overnight and simmering it again for ½ hour the next day. Rinse the wool twice and dry.

½ LB (250 G) OR ½ QT BARK FROM STEMS OR ROOTS

Recipes For Plants Used In Several Parts

SILVER BIRCH

Betula pendula or *B. populifolia*

The distinctive white- or pinkish-barked slender silver birch is common in North America, Europe, and Asia and grows well at nigh altitudes and in snowy latitudes. It is also cultivated as a garden specimen. The delicate branches bear heart-shaped leaves on a stalk, and slender, waving catkins. The bark peels off in paperlike strips and that of the larger-trunked *B. papyfera* was used for covering tepees and canoes by North American Indians. For dyeing, however, the living inner bark is better than the dead outer bark. The leaves can also be used fresh or dried for use in winter.

RECIPE FOR LEAVES

Mordant: Alum gives yellow.

Method: Put the leaves in cold water and heat slowly. Simmer for 1 hour. Strain off the leaves and cool the liquor. Enter the clean, wetted wool and return bath to the simmer. Simmer for ¾ to 1 hour. Rinse the wool twice and dry.

RECIPE FOR BARK

Mordant: Alum gives dull yellow to dull gold, iron gives purplish.

Method: Steep the bark overnight in the water to be used for dyeing. Heat slowly and simmer for 1 to 2 hours. Strain off the bark and cool the liquor. Enter the clean, wetted wool and return bath to the simmer. Simmer for ¾ to 1½ hours. Rinse the wool twice and dry.

½ LB (250G) OR ABOUT ½ PK FRESH LEAVES. INCREASE THE AMOUNT IF DRIED LEAVES ARE USED.

½ LB (250G) OR 2-4 QTS BARK, CHOPPED

ELDER

Sambucus nigra and S. canadensis

The European elder is a coarse pithy small tree common in the temperate zones of Europe. The older trees have deeply furrowed bark. The clusters of creamy white flowers (used for elder-flower wine) have a heavy scent. The leaves grow in groups of three to seven and turn yellow to purple in autumn. Besides the bark and leaves, the shining purple-black berries are also used and make a dye of great variety though not of great fastness. The elder seeds itself freely and is very fast growing, so it is worth while for a dyer to grow it for use in three or four years' time. *Sambucus canadensis* is a similar native American elder with edible purple-black berries, but it has a shrubby growth habit and delights in damp rich soil. The wide range of colors from elder is particularly pleasant and could be used in itself for an embroidery or weaving. To obtain a very dark gray, you can top-dye elder bark with walnut, as described in Chapter 6.

RECIPE FOR LEAVES

Mordant: Alum gives light yellow, chrome gives deep yellow.

Method: Young leaves give a purer color than older ones. Put the leaves in cold water and heat slowly. Simmer for ½ to 1 hour. Strain off the leaves and cool the liquor. Enter the clean, wetted wool and return to the simmer. Simmer for 15 to 30 minutes. Rinse the wool twice and dry.

1 LB (.5KG) OR 2 GALS LEAVES, BRUISED OR CHOPPED UP

RECIPE FOR BERRIES

Mordant: Alum gives violet, which can be modified by adding salt to the dyebath, or by a vinegar dip.

Method: Put the berries in cold water and heat slowly. Simmer for ½ to 1 hour. Strain off the berries and cool the liquor. Enter the clean, wetted wool and return bath to the simmer. Simmer for ½ hour or longer according to the depth of color desired. Leave the wool to steep in the bath overnight. The beautiful, violet that results can be made more blue by adding a handful of salt to the bath while the wool is steeping overnight. For a more reddish shade, dip it in the vinegar solution for a few minutes instead. Rinse the wool twice and dry.

2 LB (1KG) OR A DOZEN CLUSTERS OF BERRIES, BRUISED

A HANDFUL OF SALT
OR
VINEGAR SOLUTION OF 1 PART VINEGAR TO 2 PARTS WATER (OPTIONAL)

RECIPE FOR BARK

Mordant: Iron gives gray.

Method: Put the bark in cold water and heat slowly. Simmer for 2 hours. Strain off the bark and cool the liquor. Enter the clean, wetted wool and return bath to the simmer. Simmer for 1 to 2 hours. Rinse the wool twice and dry.

2 LBS (1KG) OR ½ PK BARK

BLACKBERRY
Rubus species

This is common wayside bush known in Scotland as bramble; some American forms are known as dewberry. It has prickly, bending stems and prickly 3- to 5-foliate leaves with white or pinkish flowers and dark fruits, most of which are edible. Gerard's *Herbal* says "They heale eies that hang out...and a decoction fastneth the teeth." There are many cultivated forms of blackberry — loganberry, himalayaberry, etc. In its wild form it grows in waste places and woodlands and quickly takes over ditches and neglected ground. On the northwest coast of the United States I found a low creeping type, which has a particularly sweet berry and also makes a good dye, as does the American black raspberry. Blackberry will also dye silk, which should be simmered at a lower temperature.

I use blackberry shoots to dye many hanks of wool a pale gray, which are then top-dyed to get subtle colors.

RECIPE FOR YOUNG SHOOTS

½ LB (250G) OR 1 PK TIPS OF YOUNG SHOOTS—ROUGHLY THE TOP 5 INCHES (THEY ARE NOT HURT BY TRIMMING)

A PINCH OF FERROUS SULFATE (FOR NEAR-BLACK)

Mordant: Alum gives gray, iron added to the dyebath gives near-black and gray-purple.

Method: Put the tips in cold water and heat slowly. Simmer for ¾ hour. Strain off the tips and cool the liquor. Enter the clean, wetted wool and return bath to the simmer. Simmer for ½ hour and test for color. A light gray-purple is obtained first, then a darker gray. For an even darker gray, add iron for the last 10 to 15 minutes of dyeing. Rinse the wool twice and dry.

RECIPE FOR BERRIES

2 LBS (1 KG) OR ABOUT 2 QTS BERRIES, CRUSHED

10-30% AMMONIA SOLUTION (FOR BLUE)

Mordant: Alum gives shades of rose. The color is not very fast.

Method: The simultaneous method of dyeing is preferable for berries. Put them in a mesh bag and enter in the bath together with the clean, wetted wool. Slowly bring bath to the simmer and simmer for ½ to 1 hour. To turn the rose color which results into blue, immediately dip the wool briefly in the ammonia solution. Rinse thoroughly and dry.

PRIVET

Ligustrum vulgare

This shrub, now somewhat naturalized in the eastern United States, is very commonly used for hedges in European and American gardens. As it needs frequent clipping, there is no problem in obtaining leaves. The dark green lanceolate leaves are small and the white flowers not conspicuous. The dark, dull, almost black berries hang on until late autumn, I grow the golden evergreen type in my garden and find that its leaves make an especially bright, rich yellow. Fresh leaves give a much better color then those even a few hours old. If you use clippings, discard the twigs — their tannin content will dull the color. This is a strong, fast dye.

RECIPE FOR LEAVES

Mordant: Alum gives dull to bright yellow, copper sulfate gives greens, and iron added to the dyebath gives dark green.

Method: Put the leaves in cold water and heat slowly. Simmer for ½ to 1 hour. Strain off the leaves and cool the liquor. Enter the clean, wetted wool and return bath to the simmer. The color should develop in about 20 minutes, but the wool can be simmered much longer to obtain a range of shades before the color begins to dull. Test the color frequently. For dark green, add iron for the last 15 minutes of dyeing. Rinse the wool twice and dry.

1 PK FRESH LEAVES SEPARATED FROM THE TWIGS

½-1 TSP FERROUS SULFATE (FOR DARK GREEN)

RECIPE FOR BERRIES

Mordant: Alum, chrome, tin and iron give many shades from pale pink to blue-purple.

Method: Put the berries and all the juice from them in cold water and heat slowly. Simmer for about ¾ hour. Strain off the berries and cool the liquor. Enter the clean, wetted wool and return bath to the simmer again. The color should develop in about 20 minutes. Many shades can be obtained by changing the proportion of berries used in relation to the amount of wool. For duller color, add iron for the last 15 minutes of dyeing. Rinse the wool twice and dry.

1 QT BERRIES OR MORE FOR DEEPER SHADES, BRUISED

A PINCH OF FERROUS SULFATE (FOR A DULLER COLOR)

LADY'S BEDSTRAW

Galium boreale or G. verum

The tiny four-petalled yellow flowers of lady's bedstraw, also called our lady's bedstraw and yellow bedstraw, make feathery tops to the soft green square stems with whorls of tiny leaves. The name recalls its use as a pleasant filling for mattresses. A common wayside flower of Europe and North America, it has a warm summer scent. It flowers in high summer, and its roots provide one of the few native British sources for red dye. It was much used in the Hebrides for the red of tartans. You can get better yellow dyes than the tops give, but if you pull up the plant to use the roots, it is satisfying to use the tops too.

RECIPE FOR TOPS

Mordant: Alum gives yellow.

Method: The simultaneous method is preferable here. Put the tops in a mesh bag and steep them overnight in the water to be used for dyeing. Enter the clean, wetted wool. Slowly bring bath to the simmer and simmer for 1 to 1½ hours. Rinse twice and dry.

1 QT OR MORE FRESHLY CUT TOPS IN FLOWER. FINELY CHOPPED

RECIPE FOR ROOTS

Mordant: Chrome gives red, alum and chrome gives light orange-red, chrome with iron added to the dyebath gives purplish red.

Method: Dig up the plants when in flower and spread them to dry for a few days. Then chop off the roots and wash them thoroughly, scrubbing them with a small brush. Chop into small pieces, put them into cold water, and heat slowly. Simmer for 1 to 2 hours. Strain off the roots and cool the liquor. Enter the clean, wetted wool and return bath to the simmer. Simmer for 1 to 2 hours. According to the color desired, add iron to the bath for the last 15 minutes of dyeing. The addition of 1½ tablespoons of vinegar for the last 15 minutes strengthens the color. Winifred Shand says that in the Hebrides the wool was washed in salty water, which I have not tried, but salt usually tends to fix dyes. Rinse the wool twice and dry.

4-6 OZ (120-180G) ROOTS

½ TSP FERROUS SULFATE (FOR PURPLISH RED)

1½ TBSP VINEGAR (OPTIONAL)

MAHONIA OR OREGON GRAPE

Mahonia aquifolium

This evergreen shrub has decorative yellow flowers and bloomy dark blue berries. It grows to 3 feet or more. The plant is native to western North America, but has long been common in Britain and is now naturalized. It is very tolerant of shade, but cannot take strong wind. The long-lasting sprays are used by florists, while the acid fruits are made into Oregon-grape jelly. A dwarf form, *M. repens,* is low and spreading and often used as ground cover in parks.

RECIPE FOR BERRIES

Mordant: None necessary, but the color is faster with a mordant. Alum gives purplish blue, which can be darkened. If no mordant is used, a tin afterbath is recommended.

Method: Put the berries in cold water and heat slowly. Simmer for ¾ hour. Strain off the berries and cool the liquor. Enter the clean, wetted wool and return bath to the simmer. Simmer for 1 hour or longer, according to the depth of color desired. If the wool was not previously mordanted, enter it in a simmering afterbath of tin and simmer for ½ hour. Wash in soapy water. Rinse twice and dry.

1 LB (.5KG) OR 1 QT OR MORE FULLY RIPE BERRIES, CRUSHED

AFTERBATH
SCANT 1 TSP STANNOUS CHLORIDE PER GAL OF WATER

RECIPE FOR ROOTS

Mordant: Alum gives buff to brown, chrome gives tan.

Method: Steep the roots overnight in the water to be used for dyeing. Heat slowly and simmer for 2 to 3 hours. Strain off the roots and cool the liquor. Enter the clean, wetted wool and return bath to the simmer. Simmer for ½ hour or longer, according to the depth of color desired. To make the color obtained with alum-mordanted wool warmer, enter the wool in a simmering afterbath of chrome and vinegar. Simmer, covered, for 10 minutes. Rinse twice and dry.

8-12 OZ (250-360G) OR ½ PK ROOTS, CHOPPED
AFTERBATH
¼ TSP POTASSIUM DICHROMATE
AND
2 TBSP VINEGAR PER GAL OF WATER

RECIPE FOR WHOLE PLANT (except berries)

Mordant: Alum gives a khaki-yellow. About 1½ times the usual amount of alum is needed. The additional alum can be added to the dyebath.

Method: Put the chopped pieces in cold water and heat slowly. Simmer for 2 to 2½ hours. Strain off the plant material and cool the liquor. Stir in the alum. Enter the clean, wetted wool and return bath to the simmer. Simmer for ½ to 1 hour. Rinse very thoroughly (because of the extra alum) and dry.

The Navajo Indians dyed wool with mahonia by just steeping it overnight, but I prefer to simmer it in the usual way.

1 LB (.5KG) OR 1 PK LEAVES, STEMS, AND ROOTS, CHOPPED AND PACKED FIRMLY

1½ TSP ALUM

RUDBECKIA OR CONEFLOWER

Rudbeckia trilobia

This biennial, common over most of the eastern and central United States, where it is well known as the brown-eyed susan, is also grown there and in Britain as a garden flower. It is an undemanding plant, with leaves that change from lobed to nearly entire as they go up the stem. It grows from 2 to 5 feet high as a coarse weed flowering from July to October. The rays, ½ to 1 inch long in the wild type, larger in the cultivated, are yellow with an orange or purple-brown base, and the disc is black-purple. It is named after two professors, father and son, of the seventeenth-eighteenth centuries. There are numerous other rudbeckias also available in the United States, some of them truly perennial.

RECIPE FOR FLOWER HEADS

Mordant: Alum gives green, chrome gives greenish gold if the whole flower head is used, warm golden yellow if only the petals are used.

Method: The simultaneous method is preferable here. Put the flower heads or petals in a mesh bag and enter in the bath together with the clean, wetted wool. Slowly bring bath to the simmer and simmer for ½ to 1 hour. Lift the bag out of the bath frequently and work the wool to keep the dyeing even. Rinse twice and dry the wool.

2 QTS FLOWER HEADS, WHOLE OR PETALS ONLY

RECIPE FOR WHOLE PLANT (except roots)

Mordant: Alum gives a pale primrose yellow.

Method: Steep the pieces overnight in the water to be used for dyeing. Heat slowly and simmer for up to 1 hour. Strain off the plant material and cool the liquor. Enter the clean, wetted wool and return bath to the simmer. Simmer for ½ to 1 hour, according to the depth of color desired. To brighten the color, add a pinch of lime to the bath for the last 15 minutes of dyeing. Lift the wool out before stirring in the lime. Rinse the wool very thoroughly (because of the lime) and dry.

½ PK WHOLE PLANTS EXCEPT ROOTS, CHOPPED ROUGHLY

A PINCH OF LIME (CALCIUM OXIDE)

BUCKTHORN

Rhamnus caroliniana, R. cathartica

R. cathartica is a common British garden shrub, and *R. caroliniana* is found over considerable stretches of the United States. Both have small greenish inconspicuous flowers and will grow treelike if not pruned. This family, one of which (Persian berries) was a traditional commercial dye, has a vast amount of dye in various parts. The twigs, the smooth grayish bark, and the berries — yellow in the Near Eastern species and red turning black in *cathartica and caroliniana* — all give a dye. I use the clippings of the plant after pruning. The berries are gathered when not quite ripe for drying, but they can also be used fresh. If they are stored, they must not be put away even slightly damp.

RECIPE FOR BERRIES OF *R. caroliniana*

Mordant: Alum and cream of tartar gives lemon yellow, alum alone gives bright yellow, chrome gives warm brown, chrome and cream of tartar gives old gold, tin gives orange, iron and cream of tartar added to the dyebath gives greenish yellow.

2-4 OZ (60-120G) BERRIES, CRUSHED
_____

½ TSP FERROUS SULFATE
AND
½ TSP CREAM OF TARTAR (FOR GREENISH YELLOW)
_____

Method: The simultaneous method is preferable for berries. Put the berries in a mesh bag and enter in the bath together with the clean, wetted wool. Slowly bring bath to the simmer and simmer for 20 to 40 minutes. Lift the bag out of the bath frequently and work the wool to keep the dyeing even. To obtain a greenish yellow, add the iron and cream of tartar for the last 15 minutes of dyeing. Rinse the wool twice and dry.

The berries of *R. cathartica* give a blue-gray with an alum mordant.

RECIPE FOR TWIGS OR BARK OF *R. cathartica*

Mordant: Alum gives brownish yellow, chrome gives brown-yellow, iron added to the dyebath gives brown.

½-1 PT STRIPPED BARK, FRESH OR DRIED, OR SMALL TWIGS, CHOPPED
_____

½ TSP FERROUS SULFATE (FOR BROWN)
_____

Method: Put the bark or twigs in cold water and heat slowly. Simmer for 1 hour. Strain off the plant material and cool the liquor. Enter the clean, wetted wool and return bath to the simmer. Simmer for 15 to 45 minutes. For brown, add iron for the last 15 minutes of dyeing. Rinse the wool twice and dry.

4. Dyes of Historic Importance

The use of dyes for fabric reaches back into history. Dyed fabric from thousands of years B.C. has been found in Egyptian tombs: indigo was grown there, and tradition holds that mummy wrappings were dyed with saffron, still occasionally used today, though most frequently in the kitchen. Madder was known in Indochina in the early centuries A.D. and indigo was grown there as well as in Persia.

The Romans used several dyes, though their most famous one, Tyrian purple, which they got from the Phoenicians, was from the *Murex,* a shellfish, not from a plant. A plum color rather than a true purple, it was worn in later centuries only as a royal and ecclesiastical privilege — no wonder, since many thousands of the *Murex* shellfish were required to make one ounce of dye.

We know little of how dyeing survived the Middle Ages, but from the evidence of paintings and illuminated manuscripts, we know that colored cloth was worn — mostly by the aristocrats — and Charlemagne passed a decree concerning the cultivation of woad, cochineal (not a plant dye), and madder.

Some of the dyes used in Anglo-Saxon England can be identified as similar to the embroidery threads of the Bayeux Tapestry: they include madder (which was imported from France), woad, and indigo. Even before the Conquest, many Norman dyers had settled in London, and a Guild of Dyers had been formed there by the end of the twelfth century. We get a glimpse of the colors of the fourteenth century from Chaucer's descriptions of the Canterbury pilgrims. The knight wore a coat and hood of green, the merchant was in motley (varicolored fabric), the wife of Bath sported red stockings, and the miller wore a white coat and a blue hood.

The development of heraldry and the great festivals of the Church encouraged the use of color symbolism. Not only in clothes and horse trappings but in banners, canopies, and flags, as we see them in the paintings of the early Renaissance and later in the works of Canaletto. This gave scope to the colorists.

Italy gained a great lead in the field of dyeing in the fourteenth century when a Florentine merchant named Federico observed the preparation and use of certain lichens for dyeing purples when he was traveling in Asia Minor. What he saw was very likely archil, until recently made from lichens in the Scottish highlands. When Federico produced the dye after experimenting in private and made his discovery known, he was rewarded with honor and privilege and given the right to use as his family name, the name Roccellia from the name of the lichen, *Roccella tinctorius*. The process of using *Roccella,* remained for some time a monopoly of Italian dyers (until one of their number brought the precious secret to England). The first European book on dyeing was published in Venice in 1429, while England had to wait until 1662 for its first published book on dyeing.

The growing trade in silk, which took such sumptuous colors, and in damasks from the East, also encouraged experimentation. Along with the spices, jewels, and songs from the East that traveled through Constantinople by dangerous caravan routes came the dye colors, with which the Europeans strove to match the vision of richness that had been opened up.

The discovery of the New World similarly meant the discovery of new dyes. Red brazilwood, which had formerly been imported from the East, was found in such quantities that its name was given to a huge country. It is fascinating to compare the English herbals of the mid-seventeenth century, such as Gerard, Culpeper, and Parkinson, with the early nineteenth-century descriptions of Rhind to see which plants originated in what parts of the world.

Some of the dyes whose history is inextricably woven into the development of European trade and agriculture can still be grown in our gardens like woad and madder, or found wild, like weld and buckthorn. Some, like indigo and logwood, cannot be found unless cultivated in temperate climes. Yet they are of such historical importance that they merit consideration and offer fascinating insights into the lives of our ancestors. So this chapter gives a fuller account of these dyes, including historical accounts of their cultivation, and practical advice on simple dye methods for today. Some of these dyes have been superseded, and one experiment will probably salve the enthusiast's curiosity. But when we take a hank of faintly yellow wool from the dye-vat and watch it turn woad-blue in the air, we can appreciate some of the excitement of a drab-clothed populace.

Since I have not been able to find brazilwood *(Caesalpina echinata)* imported in Europe or growing where I have worked in North America, I have not tested this interesting red dye. However, those who live where it is indigenous might experiment with it.

Madder, still used in many parts of the world, has been from antiquity the main plant source of red dye. But its color was equalled by two other historic dyes that come not from plants but from insects. The finest red of these was kermes, used in Syria and Phoenicia. Plutarch mentioned that kermes retained its color after 190 years, and we can see today, in museums, Coptic textiles of the fourth and fifth centuries A.D. with kermes red as fresh as if it had been dyed

BRAZILWOOD

There are several species of this family natives of South America, and of the East and West Indies. It was probably, however, first imported into Europe from the Brazils, and hence the name. Soon after its introduction, the Portuguese government began to appreciate its value, and accordingly it was made one of the objects of royal monopoly, being imported into Europe on account of the crown. From this circumstance it is known in Brazil as pao de Rainha, or Queen's wood.

When first cut, the wood is a pale red, but becomes darker by exposure to air. It is varigated with irregular and fantastical black spots, which has obtained for it among the French the name of bois de lettres.

The most permanent colours produced from this dye are those in which the natural purple red is changed by acids to an orange or yellow colour. Brazil-wood is often used in dyeing silk of a crimson hue.

Brazil-wood boiled in water communicates to it a fine red colour, while the wood itself becomes a darker colour, and if the ebullition be continued long enough the residuum will be black. Paper tinged red with this decoration is altered to a violet colour by the action of the alkalis, and to a yellow by most of the acids.

William Rhind

yesterday. Its deep red is seen in Persian and Turkish carpets, and it is still used in the countryside of Greece. The dye was used extensively in the Mediterranean and in Asia, as the kermes insects, the *Kermes ilicis,* live on the kermes oak and holm oak, which grows abundantly along the Mediterranean and in the Levant. The insects are killed with acetic acid, dried, and powdered. (The kermes insects are not to be confused with a red parasite that grows on knot grass in the sandy regions of east Germany and Poland, called "kermes berries." Inside these "berries" are blood-red worms, which are also treated with acetic acid — in the form of vinegar — and dried and ground to make a rich carmine.*)

COCHINEAL

Cochineal, the other famous red dye of history, comes from an insect that produces carminic acid, which with the appropriate mordants yields pink to carmine on wool and silk. When the Spanish arrived in Mexico in 1518, they found the Indians brushing the wingless female insects off cactus plants with fine brushes (to avoid the spikes), on to trays. The insects were then dried in the sun or over a stove and ground into a powder, and the same process is used today. Most of the pinks and carmines of ancient American embroideries are from cochineal. It is not so fast as kermes or madder, but it suffices for textiles not exposed to continual bright light.

Kermes and cochineal can still be obtained from dyehouses, and the latter in some places is a household food colorant. Cochineal is often used in combination with plant dyes, and for this reason a recipe is given here.

Cochineal also dyes silk very beautifully.

RECIPE FOR COCHINEAL

½-1 oz (15-30g) or 1½-3 tbsp COCHINEAL POWDER

½ tsp COMMON SALT

½ tsp FERROUS SULFATE (FOR VIOLET)
OR
SCANT ½ tsp STANNOUS CHLORIDE (FOR SCARLET)

Mordant: Alum gives rose to pink, chrome gives warm pink to purplish red, tin gives strong scarlet, iron added to the dyebath gives violet to gray-purple.

Method: Warm the water with the salt added to hand-heat and stir in the cochineal. Enter the clean, wetted wool and heat slowly. (It should take almost 1 hour to reach the simmer.) Then simmer for 1 hour. Add iron for violet and stir. Alternatively, for a brighter scarlet on alum-mordanted wool, leave the wool in the bath to cool and add the tin at this point. Rinse the wool twice and dry.

*This information I had from Violetta Thurston.

74

MADDER

Rubia tinctorum

The name of the madder plant is linked with the color red in many European languages, and the history of madder-growing twines in and out of the history of Europe — though the plant was also found in all of Asia and is particularly associated with Java. Pliny the Elder wrote of madder growing in the vicinity of Rome in the first century A.D., and although there are no written records, it is reasonable to suppose that its cultivation continued, for in the eighth century Charlemagne ordered it to be grown on his estates, as mentioned earlier. During the later Middle Ages it was planted on fallow fields because it needs three years to come to maturity. But madder cultivation became a fine art in Holland in the fifteenth century. The alluvial soil of the delta islands and the moist climate were ideal, and the careful patience of the Dutch in continually tilling and manuring the soil found a worthy subject in madder. We are told, "It appears to have been a peculiarity of madder growing in Holland not to sow seeds; with the painstaking care of the born gardener the Dutch madder grower trained each young plant, observing certain times hallowed by the tradition of centuries. No shoot was planted before May when the apple trees were in full bloom. The parent plants from which the shoots were taken had to be two years old. The period of growth was three years; after that the crop was taken up and an interval of ten years was allowed to lapse before madder was again planted in the soil.*

The importance of the traditional skill that fostered the cultivation of madder is underlined by the failure of the Swiss educator, Johann Pestalozzi (1746-1827), who tried his hand at it on his orphanage farm at Neuhof. His painstaking efforts and all the work of the orphans whom he cared for and taught to work for their living could not match that of his illiterate rural neighbors.

The dye resides in the root of the plant between the outer skin and the woody heart. It has to be dried and ground to a powder and, whereas the moist climate of Europe was more conducive to its growth (so that it was sometimes trained up pea-sticks), the dry, clear air of the Orient made it possible to dry it out-of-doors. Many forms of drying house were developed in Europe, and the final stage of drying was sometimes carried out by popping the roots into the baker's oven when the bread was taken out. An old Dutch print shows a horse walking in a circle strapped to a long beam that rotates a pounder, so working a heap of madder in the center. The yellow powder that results from grinding the dried root yields the greatest pigmentation if it is fermented, and for this purpose, in Europe it was kept in sealed vessels; in the Caucasus it was fermented in open pits.

The American settlers had enough to do to scrape a living in their new country for some time, and probably recipes that were known to the first colonists were never handed on. Other crops were more profitable, so despite the efforts of Thomas Jefferson and Dolly Madison to persuade farmers to cultivate dyestuffs

*G. Schaefer in CIBA Review No. 39.

MADDER

This plant is frequently mentioned by the Greek writers, who employed its root as a medicine.

The madder used for dyeing cotton in the East Indies is in some respects different from that of Europe. On the coast of Coromandel it has the name of "chat". It grows wild on the coast of Malabar; the cultivated kind is obtained from Vaour and Tuccoun, but the most esteemed is the Persian chat, called also "dumas."

It is certain that it contains at least two distinct colouring matters, a fawn and a red, and that the admixture of the former with the latter very much injures its clearness and beauty. In consequence of this, two kinds of red are obtained from madder. The first is simply called madder red, which contains the whole of the colouring matter. The other possesses far more lustre, and is much more valued: it is called Turkey red, because first obtained from the Levant. Its superior brilliancy is imparted in consequence of the red colouring matter being alone preserved; and while the tint communicated excels in brightness, it has the additional and great advantage of extreme durability.

The manner of producing this desirable effect was for a long period of time a subject of much interest and inquiry, the process used in Turkey being enveloped in mystery. Many different ingredients are used previously to applying the madder. Oil, sheep's dung, calf's blood, gall-nuts, soda, alum, and subsequently a solution of tin are employed, and the yarn undergoes seventeen distinct operations before it is finally imbued with its rich colouring. Madder has the singular property of imparting its colour to the animal fluids when given along with food. In this way it tinges the milk, urine, and even the bones, thus affording a proof that the digestive process does not in all cases destroy the natural properties of the substances taken into the stomach.

William Rhind

11

A crocheted poncho/skirt made of wool dyed with plants grown in the author's garden (weld, madder, tansy ragwort, blackberry, elder, woad, and several barks) as well as indigo.

12

Detail of poncho/skirt.

on a commercial scale, madder continued to be imported. In 1791 Coxe wrote, "the colouring ingredients have generally been such as nature handed to the thrifty housewife,"* that is, what grew wild around the homestead.

Madder was an important item of commerce for many centuries. A hundredweight of madder cost thirty shillings in the fateful year 1868, when the synthetic alizarin was produced. After this the price dropped rapidly; nevertheless, Holland and other countries continued to grow madder in considerable quantities until the Second World War, and it has continued to be a favorite of home dyers because of the shimmering brilliance of its color.

Madder needs a mordant to fix it, and alum, which had been known to the Greeks, was certainly used in Turkey in the fifteenth century and exported to Italy. The Italians soon searched for alumite within their own borders, and Pope Pius II opened the alum pits north of Rome in the mid-fifteenth century. Production was considered a monopoly of the Holy See, and when an Englishman brought workmen from these pits to Yorkshire to begin production there, they were excommunicated for taking the secret of their craft abroad.

The color, however, was duller than the bright red we associate with madder today. The brightest and most lasting dye derived from madder was Turkey red, long made by a secret process in the East and especially valued there because it dyed cotton. In this long and complicated process, the fibers were prepared by boiling, tanning, and mordanting with alum and calcium before dyeing. Dung and sumac and oak-galls, which contain tannin, were also used, Rhind tells us. Being expensive, this dye was used for embroidery threads rather than yardage. In Bali it is said that to produce a good red dye from madder takes six years.

Turkey red dyeing came to Europe from the Near East; it was probably carried to the Far East by the conquests of Islam. The Indonesians, who had obtained a kind of red dye from safflower and the annatto tree *(Bixa orellana)* adapted the process, using those plants whose bark yields alumina where aluminum was not available. I have learned how to treat madder grown in my own garden from old records.

If you dig madder up from your own plot or a friend's the roots (which should be two or preferably three years old) must be thoroughly scrubbed and then dried. Although the dye resides mainly between the outer skin and woody center of the plant, these are so hard to separate that I use the whole root.

You can make a drying rack by stretching fine wire mesh or muslin over a rough wooden frame or an old picture frame; hang this above the kitchen stove or in another warm place. Turn the roots over occasionally, and when they are dry, cut them up roughly and finish off the drying in a warm oven. Then grind these pieces with a mortar and pestle, or in a coffee grinder.

Since many dyers will use commercial madder, a more pure form that can be obtained from a dye-house, rather than growing their own, I give quantities for this as well as for madder roots in the following recipes.

*Quoted in Rita J. Adrosko, *Natural Dyes in the United States*, 1968.

RECIPE FOR RED

Mordant: Alum gives Chinese lacquer red, chrome gives garnet red, tin gives orange-red.

2 oz (60 G) or 3-4 tbsp commercially produced madder powder or at least 3 times this amount of chopped roots

1 gal *hard* water

Method: Some dyers steep the madder overnight in the water to be used for dyeing. If you are using powder, add it to the water and stir; if you use roots, put them in a mesh bag and enter together with the clean, wetted wool. It is very important to heat the bath very slowly — it should take 1 to 2 hours to reach the simmer. Do not allow the bath to get above simmering point, as the yellow color is extracted at the higher temperatures. For garnet red, keep an even lower temperature — below 140°F. (60°C.). Simmer the wool for 30 to 40 minutes after it reaches the simmer. Leave the wool in the bath to cool. Rinse the wool once thoroughly, then wash in soapy water, rinse twice and dry.

RECIPE FOR ORANGE

¼-½ oz (7-15 G) or 6-10 tsp commercial madder or 3 times this amount of chopped roots

1 tsp cream of tartar (optional)

1 gal *hard* water
or
1 gal liquor from a yellow dyestuff such as onion skins or weld

Mordant: Tin gives pure orange.

Method: If you are using powder, add it to the water or liquor and stir well; if you are using roots, put them in a mesh bag. The cream of tartar may be added at this point to brighten the color. Enter the clean, wetted wool. It is very important to heat the bath very slowly — it should take 1 to 2 hours to reach the boiling point. Boil the wool for 40 minutes. Let the wool cool in the bath. Wash in soapy water. Rinse twice and dry.

WOAD

Isatis finctoria

The knowledge of dyeing with woad undoubtedly survived through the Middle Ages. Among the earliest records of this dye is mention of a woad market in the district of Cologne in the thirteenth century, and after that time the craft was in the hands of various guilds. The medieval guilds existed for the mutual aid and protection of members and crafts, but the dyers in the Wool Guild of Florence, among whom the woad dyers were the chief, were oppressed and given only minor membership. As a result, they fought a long battle for better conditions with, according to J.B. Hurry, "every weapon which in modern times has been resorted to in conflicts between capital and labour."* Their fraternity, which had started as the Guild of St. James, came under the protection of Saint Nicholas, probably because so much of the trade was carried by sea. Richard Hakluyt, the English geographer whose *Principall Navigations, Voiages, and Discoveries of the English Nation* was published in 1589, wrote:

The marchaundy of Brabant and Zeeland

Be madre [madder] and woade, that dyers take one hande

To dyen withe garleke and onyons,

And saltfyshe als for husbond and commons.

Hakluyt also speaks of Genoese merchants coming to England in great carracks with black pepper "and of woade grete plante,...coton, roche-alum," etc., and taking in exchange English "wollene clothe of colours all."

Flemish weavers and dyers who had earlier established themselves in Lincolnshire and East Anglia found woad a lucrative crop in the sixteenth century, when clothing was ostentatious and extravagant, and blue was a fashionable color. Three pieces of cloth required a barrel of woad, and a burgher's wife might pay as much for one dress as would buy a small house.

The preparation of the dye demanded fermentation, and it is said that Queen Elizabeth would not travel near the woad towns because of the stench; a decree forbade processing woad within five miles of the royal estates!

In the seventeenth century, the Dutch East India Company imported quantities of indigo into Europe, and in spite of many attempts to exclude it, by the middle of the century indigo had superseded woad as the chief blue dye in England. Woad continued to be grown, however, since it was used to aid fermentation in the indigo vats, and this humble plant still contributes color to English life as an ingredient in the blue uniforms of the London police.

Woad also provided the beautiful blue pigment of European painting from the thirteenth century on, and one of the most popular subjects of medieval and Early Renaissance art — the Virgin Mary — was traditionally clad in a robe that glowed pale or dark blue with the juice of this plant. (The scum that rose to the top of the dye vat was mixed with plaster of Paris and white of egg for the pale shades; the plant was bruised with vinegar and urine and set in the sun to make the darker shades. **)

*J.B. Hurry, *The Woad Plant*.

**Quoted by Violetta Thurston in an article in the *Journal of Weavers, Spinners, and Dyer's of Great Britain*.

WOAD

This plant was at a very early period employed as a colouring matter by the ancient Britons. It was anciently called glastum from the Celtic word glas, blue, whence Glastonbury derived its name. The ancient Britons, when first invaded by the Romans, were in the practice of staining their bodies of a blue colour with some preparation of this substance; thence also is supposed to be derived the name Briton from the celtic britho, paint.

The two first gatherings render the best woad. The plants are mowed down with a scythe, and as soon as collected are washed in a stream of water, and dried in the sun. The desiccation must be rapidly performed. Immediately on being dried from the effects of the washing, it is conveyed to a mill, resembling the oil or tan mills, and is ground into a smooth paste. A blackish crust is soon formed on the outside, which, if it happen to crack, is carefully reunited. Should this be neglected little worms would be produced in the cracks, and the woad lose part of its strength. After remaining thus covered a fortnight, the heaps are opened, and the crust rubbed and mixed with the inside. This matter is then formed into solid balls.

These balls require a farther preparation before they can be converted to the purpose of dyeing. They are first beated with wooden mallets on a brick or stone floor, until they are reduced to coarse powder. This is heaped up into the middle of the apartment to the height of about four feet, space being left to allow a sufficient passage round the sides; it is then moistened with water, which speedily induces fermentation, and thick fetid fumes are emitted. The heap is daily moistened and stirred about with shovels, for the space of twelve days, after which period it is moved less frequently, and without being watered. At length it is made into a heap for the dyer. The proper mode of conducting the fermentation, and the exact time at which it ought to be stopped, still remain so uncertain, that those who make it their business to prepare woad have no decided facts or indications to govern their management in this respect; and the goodness of any particular quantity can never be ascertained otherwise than by actual use.

William Rhind

One of the first concrete facts of English history which a child learns at school is that the Ancient Britons dyed themselves blue with a plant called Woad.

Did the Ancient Britons really dye themselves blue? Caesar clearly says they did: "All the Britons stain themselves with Woad (vitrum), which produces a blue colour and gives them a more horrible appearance in battle." Pliny says, however, "There is a plant like Plantain, called in Gaul glastum, with

Continued overleaf

which the wives and daughters of the Britons smear their bodies in certain ceremonies and go naked, being of the colour of Ethiopians;" while Ovid speaks of our ancestors as Virides (green) Britannos. Lastly, Herodian refers to the Ancient Britons as being ignorant of the use of clothes, but "They mark their bodies with various figures of all kinds of animals, which is the reason they wear no clothes for fear of hiding these figures."

Caesar and Pliny, then, agree as to the use of Woad as a decorative pigment, but Caesar says it was blue, Pliny that it was black, while Ovid, although not mentioning the exact substance, refers to our ancestors as "green", and Herodian intimates that they were tattooed. It is quite possible that each of these writers is more or less correct, for Woad will yield not only a blue pigment — which, however, is often more or less green — but even more easily yields a black one, as the hands of the Woad gatherers in autumn plainly show.

To return to our ancestors.

(1) They may have dyed themselves blue by infusing fresh young Woad leaves in hot water, adding pearl ash or wood ashes, and washing themselves with the liquid.

(2) By substituting an excess of lime-water or by slaking quicklime in the infusion, they might have dyed themselves a green colour.

(3) By rubbing themselves with the juice of the plant they would have dyed themselves as black as the "wadmen" still dye their hands every autumn when cropping and balling the Woad.

(4) By infusing the plant, adding a small quantity of lime water, and drying the precipitate they could have obtained nearly pure indigo with which (a) they could have tattooed themselves, or (b) smeared it on their bodies, mixed with oil.

(5) It is most likely, however, that they obtained woad-indigo and used it for tattooing their bodies from the scum which rises to the top of the vessel in which the process of Woad dyeing is being successfully carried on. This was probably the source from which Pliny's chalk was stained blue, as it was that from which the missal illuminators of mediaeval times — the pictori that Ruellius speaks of — obtained their beautiful blue pigment.

"Woad as a Prehistoric Pigment." By Charles B. Plowright, M.D., in the Journal of the Royal Horticultural Society, 1901.

½ LB (250G) YOUNG, FRESH LEAVES OR MORE—ENOUGH TO FILL THE VESSEL USED, WHICH MUST HAVE A SCREW TOP

¼ OZ (6G) OR ABOUT 2 TSP LIME (CALCIUM OXIDE)
OR
A FEW TBSP LIQUID AMMONIA (THE AMOUNT DEPENDS ON THE SIZE OF THE CONTAINER)

A GENEROUS PINCH OF BRAN, IF AVAILABLE

Woad prefers a rich, limy soil and still grows in England, especially in East Anglia, as an escape from the old woad fields. A biennial herb of the family Cruciferae, it bears small yellow flowers with its characteristic four petals on top of a thin stem, two to five feet high. The leaves, which resemble light green spinach, grow in a rosette on the ground and most of the way up the stem. They last through the winter in my garden, but the best to pick for dye are the succulent young leaves, about six to eighteen inches high in June or July. These will be replaced by new growth.

The plants are reproduced from the brownish purple pendulous pods, which are dispersed by the wind in nature. For cultivation, these should be soaked overnight before sowing in the husk. They are planted about two inches underground from February to midsummer. Woad needs to be kept weed-free (it was one of the earliest crops to be given such care in England) and to be thinned out to eight to ten inches.

Some enthusiasts may want to try the old fermentation method described by Rhind and risk the "foul oders" so repugnant to Queen Elizabeth, but I use a simple contemporary method to extract the dye, even if it is not so strong or so fast. A large jar with a screw top is needed and a glass rod for stirring.

RECIPE FOR WOAD

Mordant: None necessary.

Method: Pack the leaves in the jar, pressing down very tightly. Pour over water heated to just under boiling point and continue to press down the leaves until the jar is full, so no air remains when the top is screwed on. Keep this at about 100° F. (40°-60° C.) for 6 to 12 hours. Allow to cool until you can see small bubbles rising. Open the jar and stir in the lime or the ammonia with a glass rod, which will generate ammonia gas. The yellowish liquid will begin to turn greenish yellow. Now enter the clean, wetted wool. The liquor should overflow so the jar can be topped without any air entering. Steep the wool for 1 hour. Lift the wool out with the glass rod, and it will turn pale blue in contact with the air. It can be immersed again, and left another ½ hour in the topped jar. On lifting it out, again the color will become deeper. This may be repeated until the bath is exhausted. As the liquor loses strength, add a generous pinch of bran to reactivate the fermentation. Steep the wool another ½ hour. Then add another 2 teaspoons of lime, and steep the wool again. This cycle of adding bran and lime can be repeated until all the dye substance has been exhausted.

INDIGO

Indigofera tinctoria

It was certainly in very ancient times that men discovered the strange fact that the yellow juices of the indigo shrub would dye blue on wool, cotton, and many other fibers. The plant, whose use was highly developed in the Orient by Marco Polo's time, was cultivated for its dye centuries before Christ, and indigo-dyed textiles that still hold their color have been found in Egyptian tombs and in the Inca graves of Peru, as well as from ancient India.

Although woad makes a faster dye, it is not so bright or clear as indigo, which was much sought after when it was introduced into Europe by the Dutch in the sixteenth century. Until about 1670, the English sent their bolts of white cloth to Holland to be dyed, but then an enterprising Dutch dyer set up a workshop and taught indigo-dyeing to the English.

The French were also skilled dyers; like the Dutch they excelled in making marvelous tapestries that covered the drafty walls of their palaces. (The art of tapestry has recently been revitalized in France by the discovery that it is not an unlimited but a deliberately *limited* range of carefully chosen colors that gives tapestry its beauty.) During the Napoleonic wars, when trade with the East was halted and indigo became scarce, the French government offered a reward for the discovery of a new dye that could be cultivated in Europe. But nothing better was found than the old method of "bottoming" with woad for fastness and "topping" with the precious indigo for brightness.

Indigo is an excellent dye for cotton as well as wool. The marvelous cloths of Nigeria are still dyed in great indigo vats in the ground, and often tie-dyed, a form of decoration that exploits the grading of the different shades of blue. A few artist-craftsmen work as tie-dyers in this medium today.

According to the way it is used, indigo produces a variety of blues, yet they are so distinctive that one readily recognizes the plant source. A dye book of 1669 gives the following musical description of the shades: "White blue, pearly blue, faint blue, delicate blue, sky blue, Queen's blue, King's blue, garter blue, infernal blue."

When you buy indigo, specify "genuine natural indigo." If you use a synthetic indigo, which is much stronger, use only a quarter of the quantity called for in the recipes. Store indigo in a tightly closed jar or can since it does tend to get a little damp, making weight and volume measurement difficult.

Indigo differs from all other dyes described in this book because it is not soluble in water, which is the most convenient medium to penetrate the fibers we deal with. So the indigo is "reduced" — that is, the oxygen is removed from it with sodium hydrosulfite — and it is changed into a substance called "indigo white," which will dissolve in an alkali, in this case a caustic-soda solution. In this state it is a yellowish liquid. After this has impregnated the fiber, the indigo white is oxygenated again by exposure to the air, becoming indigo blue. Since this is insoluble in water, it will not wash out. Because alkalis such as caustic soda are not good for wool, the minimum necessary should be used. Extreme fastness is obtained by slow dips in the solution followed by exposing the fibers

INDIGO

There are not less than twenty-four species of this genus enumerated, all natives of tropical climates. In Hindostan, China, Japan, the southern parts of Africa, America, Java, and Madagascar, the various species of this plant grow in a wild state.

The real nature of indigo was not generally known in Europe until a long period after it had been obtained direct from India, the country of its production, and many erroneous notions existed as to its nature at a comparatively recent period. In the letters patent granted to the proprietors of mines in the principality of Halberstadst, not many centuries ago, indigo was classed among the minerals, to obtain which the works were permitted to be erected.

Marco Polo, indeed, who flourished in the thirteenth century, and who is the earliest European traveller into China and India on record, relates that he saw indigo made in the kingdom of Coulan, and describes the process by which it was prepared. "Indigo", says the old Venetian, "of excellent quality and large quantities, is made here (Coulan). They procure it from an herbaceous plant, which is taken up by the roots and put into tubs of water, where it is suffered to remain till it rots, when they press out the juice. This upon being exposed to the sun, and evaporated, leaves a kind of paste, which is cut into small pieces of the form in which to see it brought to us.

William Rhind

A student of the author, preparing to dip cloth in an indigo vat. Behind her, already dyed yardage hangs on a line to dry.

to the air for four, ten, or twenty dips. (Persians give as many as forty dips for fine work.) A more vivid color comes with a few stronger dips.

It is not easy to make indigo dye so fast that it does not rub off just a little on the skin. This does not matter if one's skin is dark, and African women test cloth by rubbing it on their wrists to see if it is their traditional indigo and not a synthetic.

Several of the substances used are dangerous and you must take great care with them, especially in a household where there are children. It is wise to wear a rubber or heavy plastic apron, and rubber gloves. You will also need a good supply of newspaper and an old blanket, if possible. (The process is messy and should be done out-of-doors or in a shed, or on a floor well protected by newspaper.) A thermometer, glass rod, a glass or stoneware vessel, and a large plastic or galvanized metal tub (with a cloth or lid to cover it) that will hold 12 gallons are necessary.

Since few people will want to go to the trouble of setting up an indigo vat for only 4 ounces of wool, and since most dyers will want to seize the opportunity of "bottoming" or first-dyeing fibers for later experiments in top-dyeing, the quantities given here are for *four times the usual* — that is, they are for 1 pound of wool (or cotton), either fiber or cloth, and 12 gallons of water. The recipe may be halved, however, to make a 6-gallon vat. Fiber should be tied with string in the usual way; cloth should have holding strings attached at two corners. Both need to be weighted at the bottom to prevent them from floating on the surface of the dye.

The recipe below is not simple but the resulting dye is faster than that obtained by an easier method. Indigo extract may be bought, but indigo grains are much better. Since several of the substances used absorb moisture and their weight by volume therefore varies, the quantities are given here by volume only.

Note: The recipe given is for 1 pound of cotton or wool (lye is not good for wool but if I am dyeing cotton, I put in small quantities of wool for embroidery or weaving) and 12 gallons of water.

2½ CUPS SEA SALT OR COMMON SALT
1 CUP LYE FLAKES (SODIUM HYDROXIDE)
SCANT 1 CUP SODIUM HYDROSULFITE (ALSO CALLED DIOTHONITE) PLUS ABOUT A QUARTER OF THIS AMOUNT MORE FOR ADJUSTING THE SOLUTION
1 CUP INDIGO GRAINS
3 QTS SOFT WATER

RECIPE FOR INDIGO

INDIGO-HYDROSULFITE STOCK SOLUTION

Method: Put the water, warmed to approximately 120°F. (49°C.) into a stoneware or glass vessel and add slowly, stirring carefully, the salt, lye, and sodium hydrosulfite, in that order. Allow each to dissolve before adding the next. When they are thoroughly dissolved, add the indigo a little at a time, again stirring carefully. Leave this to stand overnight or longer. Before using, test it by dipping in a glass rod, which should come out dripping a clear pale yellow liquid. If there are solid blue specks in the liquid or if the liquid has a greenish tinge, all the indigo has not been reduced. Add additional teaspoons of hydrosulfite and stir gently until you obtain a clear pale yellow.

INDIGO-HYDROSULFITE DYE VAT

Method: Set the vat on newspapers and wrap a blanket or more newspapers around it and tie them securely. The covering provides insulation to maintain the temperature. (I usually use a galvanized metal vat placed on two bricks in my garden, and make a small fire under the vat each day to warm the bath. In this case, of course, one does not need to wrap the vat up.) Fill the vat ¾ full with water that is about 120°-130°F. (49°-55°C.)

Note: The vat must *never* be heated above 140°F. (60°C.) or the dye will be spoiled, and should be kept at about 120°F. (49°C.) or cooler.

Sprinkle in the hydrosulfite and stir gently. (This hydrosulfite is to remove the oxygen from the water.) Leave to settle for 15 to 30 minutes. Then, *with rubber gloves on,* lower the container of indigo-hydrosulfite solution, held upright, under the surface of the warm water. Do this gently so that no bubbles are formed. Allow the liquids to meet and tip the stock solution container gently over so the liquids flow into each other. Do not allow air to get into the vat (you have just gone to a lot of trouble to extract all the oxygen). Cover the vat closely with a cloth or lid — or both — and leave to settle for at least ½ hour. Then test with a glass rod to see if the solution is clear yellow. If it is greenish, add a tablespoon of hydrosulfite; if there are white specks on the rod, add some lye flakes dissolved in water. Holding the clean, wetted fiber or cloth by the attached strings, lower it gently into the bath at the side of the vat so the weights carry it under the surface.(Some people dip the fiber in very mild detergent and rinse before dipping, but I simply wet it.) Keep it there, moving gently for 1 to 5 minutes. (Many dips and airings give a faster color than the color achieved in one dip.) *Do not let it drip into the vat* — hold it over the floor (hence the newspapers). The dripping solution, already oxidizing, would carry oxygen back into the vat.

The fiber will come out of the vat a faint yellow and will turn blue in the air in a few minutes. You can dip it any number of times so long as you let it hang in the air until it blues between dips. If the vat begins to turn greenish, it indicates that it is becoming exhausted of dye or air is getting in. A tablespoon of hydrosulfite allowed to settle in it for 15 minutes may revive it. Finally, the fiber should be hung by its holding strings, still weighted, on a line until it dries. Then wash in soapy water, rinse very thoroughly, and dry.

Pour the exhausted vat solution into a pit — not a river or drain — to avoid pollution.

---

1 TBSP SODIUM HYDROSULFITE

THE STOCK SOLUTION, PREPARED BEFOREHAND

---

12 GALS SOFT WATER

---

1 TBSP SODIUM HYDROSULFITE
OR
2/3 TSP LYE FLAKES, IF NECESSARY

LOGWOOD

Haematoxylon campechianum

The logwood tree, also called campeachy wood, blackwood, and *bois bleu* or *blauholz,* grows in Central America and northern South America. It was taken from Campeachy on the Gulf of Mexico and successfully propagated in the West Indies. By 1671 at least it was used in the American colonies. In 1731 Mark Catesby, an eighteenth-century naturalist who traveled in the United States, lamented the "bloody disputes which this useful tree has occasioned between the Spaniards and the English,"* and expressed a wish that the American colonists would propagate it.

The trees were cut into logs several feet long and the outer parts were chipped away to leave the valuable red core. It was a useful cargo because it could serve as ballast. The logs were sold to apothecaries, who rasped or chipped the wood, allowed it to ferment in water for some days, and then boiled it to make dye liquor.

The tree, which reaches 30 to 45 feet in height, grows very rapidly in marshy ground and matures in a few years. The bark is rough, dark brown, and the racemes of yellow flowers are followed by double-valved pods with kidney-shaped seeds.

Although as its name indicates, logwood gives a bluish or purple color, this does not retain its brightness, and it has always been used chiefly as one of the ingredients of a black dye.

Today logwood can be obtained in the form of chips from dye houses, and is not expensive.

RECIPE FOR LOGWOOD

Mordant: Alum gives violet to gray, tin gives purple, chrome gives gray to near black, and iron added to the dyebath gives dark gray to near black.

Method: For bright colors, put the chips in cold water and heat to hand-heat. Enter the clean, wetted wool and slowly bring the bath to just under boiling point, stirring constantly. Cool, rinse the wool, and shake out the chips when it is dry.

For dull colors, put the chips in cold water and heat slowly. Simmer for up to 3 hours — the longer they simmer, the stronger and duller the color. Strain off the chips and cool the liquor. If you want to obtain a good warm dark gray, use chrome-mordanted wool and add acetic acid or vinegar to the bath. The addition of some cutch or walnut liquor will deepen the color.(If you have none previously bottled, use cutch or rotten black walnuts in the quantity given here.) Enter the clean, wetted wool and return bath to the simmer. Simmer for 1 hour or longer. If you are using iron to darken the color, add it for the last 15 minutes of dyeing. Rinse the wool twice and dry.

LOGWOOD

This tree was first discovered in the bays of Campeachy and Honduras, growing in the greatest luxuriance and abundance. It was known as a dye-wood as early as the reign of Elizabeth, but its use was forbidden by an act of parliament for "abolishing certain deceitful stuffs employed in dyeing cloths." The prohibition was continued until the year 1661, the words of the act by which it was then repealed stating "that the ingenious industry of these times hath taught the dyers of England the art of fixing colours made of logwood; so that by experience they are found as lasting and serviceable as the colour made with any other sort of dye-wood."

The logwood-tree grows abundantly throughout whole districts in Jamaica. Besides being cultivated as a dye-wood it is used for other purposes. It is found well adapted for making strong full hedges, and is constantly planted for this purpose, no other fences being seen in many parts of the island. It is excellent for fuel, and, according to Dampier, is advantageously used in hardening or tempering steel. The wood of this tree is very hard and heavy; it is of a deep orange red colour; it yields its colour both to aqueous and spirituous menstruae, but the latter extracts it the most readily and copiously. A decoction of this wood is of deep violet or purple colour, which after a time changes to a yellowish tint, and becomes finally black.

William Rhind

½-1 oz (15-30G) LOGWOOD CHIPS, ACCORDING TO DEPTH OF SHADE DESIRED

1½ TBSP ACETIC ACID

OR

4 TBSP VINEGAR (FOR WARM GRAY WITH CHROME)

1½-1¾ TBSP CUTCH EXTRACT

OR

4-5 ROTTEN BLACK WALNUT HULLS (FOR NEAR BLACK)

½ TSP FERROUS SULFATE (FOR DARK GRAY)

---

*From *Natural History of Carolina, Florida and the Bahama Islands,* London, 1771.

SAFFLOWER
Carthamus tinctorius

This plant is also known as bastard saffron, false saffron, American saffron, dyer's saffron, distaff thistle, and dyer's thistle. (It is not related to *Crocus sativus,* commonly called "saffron," though both are used for yellow dye.) Safflower, long cultivated in India, China, and Egypt as well as southern Europe, is of unknown origin. It is included here more for its historical interest than its usefulness. This was the dye used to bind legal documents — the pinkish red of "red tape." It is still used in the manufacture of rouge and lipsticks, as, Rhind reminds us, it was by the ancient Chinese. It is also used for coloring liqueurs.

To obtain the red dye for which safflower was treasured, particularly as a silk dye, it is necessary to wash out the yellow dye, which is soluble in water. This used to be done by men who treaded the florets in a trough of water. Alum, potash, cream of tartar, and citric acid were all used to bring out the color, which could vary from bright orange through poppy to rose.

Safflower is an annual plant that grows two to three feet high and has a whitish stem, upright but branching near the top. It has oval, spiny, sharp-pointed leaves with bases clasping around the stem. The orange-yellow flower head is like a thistle, and it is from this part that the dye is extracted. Gather the flowers as they open, without waiting for the whole head to ripen, because when they are fully blown, the brilliance of the color is fading. The color also deteriorates with damp. Dry the flowers in the shade.

Safflower is also made into an extract, but I have not been able to obtain it.

The following recipe is for a dull yellow; the red is too complicated to obtain.

RECIPE FOR SAFFLOWER

Mordant: Alum gives yellow.

Method: Put the florets in cold water and heat slowly. Simmer for ½ to 1 hour. Strain off the florets and cool the liquor. Enter the clean, wetted wool and return to the simmer. Simmer for 1 hour. Rinse the wool twice and dry.

SAFFLOWER

This plant is a native of Egypt, and the warmer climates of Asia. It is likewise cultivated in the Levant and the southern parts of Europe. The Chinese have long known its use, and produce from it their finest red. The colour called by them bing, which is used by the Japanese ladies as a cosmetic, is made from it, and kept in little round procelain cups. "With this," says Thunberg, "they paint, not their cheeks, as the Europeans do, but their lips. If the paint is very thin, the lips appear red; but if it be laid on thick, they become of violet hue, which is here considered as the greatest beauty."

We obtain it from the East Indies and from Turkey, that from India being considered the most valuable. It is cultivated with success in the gardens of France, but not as an article of commerce. In Spain it is grown in gardens as marygolds are in England, to colour soups, olives, and other dishes.

A smaller variety of the carthamus is cultivated in Egypt, where it forms a considerable article of commerce, "the dyes the Egyptians use," says Volney, "are probably as old as the time of the Tyrians, and they carry them at this day to a perfection not unworthy that people; but their workmen, jealous of the art, make an impenetrable mystery of the process." Hasselquist, in his Voyage d'Egypte, describes the manner in which the Egyptians prepare the carthamus for use.

Safflower is imported into England from India and Turkey: the Indian is very much superior.

In Germany this plant is cultivated pretty extensively on light land well pulverized. It is sown in rows about eighteen inches distance, and afterwards thinned to three or four inches apart in the row. In September the plants begin to flower, and the field is then gone over once a week, for six or seven weeks, to gather the expanded florets, which are dried in a kiln in the same manner as true saffron. Turkeys and geese are said to feed greedily on the seed, and soon fatten on it.

William Rhind

½ LB (250G) OR 1 PT FRESH FLORETS,
PRESSED DOWN FIRMLY

½ oz (14ɢ) FUSTIC CHIPS

or

⅛ oz (3.5ɢ) or ½ TSP FUSTIC EXTRACT

FUSTIC

Chlorophora tinctoria

The fustic tree is tall and branching and has smooth, oval leaves. The wood is a sulfur-yellow color with orange veins, and the knotty parts make the best dye.

Since the yellow fustic gives is not as bright as that from weld or buckthorn, and both of these are easily available, it has usually been used for compound colors, especially with indigo to make "Saxon green" and mordanted with chrome to make "drab." Our ancestors must have often had to be content with the dull colors described by "fustian," and they must have welcomed clear bright colors for contrast.

Fustic is available from dye houses in the form of chips, and is also made up as an extract, which I have not been able to obtain.

RECIPE FOR FUSTIC

Mordant: None necessary, but the dye can be made much more fast with a mordant. Chrome gives warm yellow, alum gives lemon yellow, and tin gives a bright yellow which is less fast. Alum should be used if the yellow is to be overdyed for olive greens.

Method: If you use chips, steep them overnight in the water to be used for dyeing; if you use extract, dissolve it in the water and heat slowly. Simmer 1 hour for bright colors and up to 3 hours for dull colors. Strain off the chips, if used, and cool the liquor. Enter the clean, wetted wool and return bath to the simmer. Simmer for 30 minutes; longer will dull the color. Rinse the wool twice and dry.

5. Dyes for Cotton, Linen, and Silk

Wool has much more affinity for plant dyes than any other natural fiber, and it is for wool that most dyes are developed during the past centuries (though there are probably many dyes for cottons developed by the American Indians and in Africa and Asia that have not been recorded). So most of the recipes in this book are for wool. In addition, since cotton dyeing is more complicated and less satisfactory, the beginner is advised to experiment with wool. Nevertheless, because in some places cotton may be more convenient than wool, this chapter deals with some of the plants that dye cotton, and some dyes that are especially suitable for linen and silk are mentioned.

Most cotton sold in hanks or skeins for crochet and embroidery will already have been scoured and bleached, or offered in its natural cotton color, which is a pleasant base for dyes. So most readers will not be concerned with the following paragraphs and will proceed to mordant. Mordanting is very important with cotton dyeing. Recipes for cotton and linen mordants are given below. For those who work with less fully prepared cotton fiber, however, the following notes are given.

SCOURING COTTON

To remove before dyeing any natural wax or other substance left in 4 ounces (120 grams) of cotton, put the cotton in soft water, heat, and boil for 1 hour. Rinse the cotton, and then boil it for 1 to 1½ hours in 1 gallon of soft water in which 1 cup of soft soap (see page 17) or 1 tablespoon soapflakes and ½ teaspoon washing soda have been dissolved. Rinse thoroughly.

BLEACHING COTTON AND LINEN

To bleach natural cotton for dyeing very pale colors, or to bleach linen, use a bath of common household chlorine bleach in the proportions given by the manufacturer. Or mix 2 tablespoons of chloride of lime with a cup of soft water, allow the sediment to settle, and add the clear liquid to the bleach bath. Soak the cotton in the bath for 2 to 3 hours, stirring occasionally. Then hang the fiber in the sun to air for a few hours. Repeat the soaking and airing until the fiber is white enough.

The soapwort plant *(Saponaria officinalis)* was used traditionally as a gentle bleach and cleaner, and is still used for extremely delicate fibers, but the process is too lengthy for the dyer's use.

MORDANTING COTTON AND LINEN

Mordanting silk is discussed at the end of this chapter. A few dyes, such as walnut, will dye cotton without a mordant, but mordanting is generally important with cotton. For mordanting the fiber must be clean, and it should be wetted. Unlike wool and silk, cotton and linen may be boiled.

The following recipes are for 4 ounces of cotton and 1 gallon of water. Soft water is preferable. The first recipe is practical for most purposes, but serious dyers will want to use the more thorough method.

4 OZ (120G) COTTON, LINEN, OR MIXTURES MAINLY OF THESE FIBERS

2 OZ (60G) OR 3 TBSP ALUM

2½ OZ (75G) OR 1½ TBSP POWDERED OAK GALLS, GROUND IN HOUSEHOLD GRINDER
OR
LIQUOR FROM 2 OZ (60G) OR A LARGE HANDFUL SUMAC LEAVES BOILED IN A LITTLE WATER FOR ½ HOUR AND STRAINED
OR
¼ OZ (7G) OR 1½ TSP TANNIC ACID

¼ OZ (7G) OR 2 TSP WASHING SODA

TO MORDANT COTTON AND LINEN WITH ALUM-TANNIN — A QUICK METHOD

Method: Dissolve the alum and soda in a little boiling water and add to the rest of the water. Enter the clean, wetted fiber. Slowly bring the bath to the boiling point, stirring occasionally, and boil the fiber for 1 hour. Let bath cool a little and add the oak galls or tannic acid dissolved in a little water, or the sumac liquor. Keep bath at the simmer for 1 hour. Stir from time to time. Leave the fiber to cool in the bath overnight. In the morning, remove the fiber, squeeze out the excess water, and rinse. Dye the fiber immediately, or dry and store in a dry place for future use.

TO MORDANT COTTON AND LINEN WITH ALUM-SODA

4 OZ (120G) COTTON, LINEN, OR MIXTURES MAINLY OF THESE FIBERS

1 OZ (30G) (1½ TBSP) ALUM

¼ OZ (7G) (2 TSP) WASHING SODA

Method: Dissolve the alum and soda in a little boiling water and add to the rest of the water. Enter the clean, wetted fiber. Slowly bring the bath to the boiling point, stirring occasionally, and boil the fiber for 1 hour. Leave the fiber in the bath overnight. In the morning, remove the fiber and squeeze out the excess water. Dye the fiber immediately, or wrap in a towel, dry in a warm place, and store for future use.

TO MORDANT COTTON AND LINEN WITH ALUM-TANNIN-ALUM — TRADITIONAL METHOD

Method: Begin exactly as in the preceding recipe for alum-soda, again leaving the fiber to cool in the bath overnight. In the morning, make a fresh bath with the powdered oak galls or liquor from sumac leaves. Enter the cotton, and bring to the boil. Boil for 1 hour. Leave the fiber to cool in the bath overnight again. In the morning, remove the fiber, squeeze slightly, and rinse. Then prepare a second alum-soda bath, enter the fiber, and again bring to the boiling point. Boil the fiber for 1 hour and leave to cool in the bath overnight again. In the morning, remove the fiber, squeeze out the excess water, and rinse. Dye the fiber immediately or dry and store in a dry place for future use.

Some plants can only be used at one season, or are better used then, so I have arranged the recipes seasonally again. Under the Winter heading are dyes that are in a dried form or in chips or extracts, which can be used at any time. In this way, some range of color, even if much more limited than with wool, can be obtained with cotton in any season.

4 OZ (120G) COTTON

NOTE: *TWICE THE FOLLOWING QUANTITIES OF ALUM AND SODA WILL BE NEEDED, AS TWO BATHS ARE REQUIRED.*

1 OZ (30G) OR 1½ TBSP ALUM

¼ OZ (7G) OR 2 TSP WASHING SODA

2½ OZ POWDERED OAK GALLS, GROUND IN HOUSEHOLD GRINDER
OR
2 OZ (60G) OR A LARGE HANDFUL SUMAC LEAVES

Recipe for Spring

SMARTWEED

Polygonum hydropiper

This nearly glabrous, erect annual weed of the northern hemisphere is found in dampish ground. It grows to about 2 feet and has tiny pedicules of greenish flowers. It is burning to the taste; it is also known as water-pepper. In the eighteenth century it was considered the most durable yellow dye in parts of the United States where weld was not available. It is very color fast. Smartweed is also suitable for wool mordanted with alum or chrome.

Mordant: Alum-tannin-alum gives yellow to gold.

Method: Steep the plant for a few days in the water to be used for dyeing. Heat slowly and simmer for just a few minutes. Reduce the temperature slightly and cook for ½ hour more. Strain off the plant material and enter the clean, wetted cotton. Bring the bath to just under the boiling point and keep at this temperature for 1 hour. For a stronger color, leave the cotton in the bath to cool. Rinse the cotton and dry.

2 QTS WHOLE PLANTS EXCEPT ROOTS, CHOPPED

Recipes for Summer

REEDS
Phragmites species

BROOMSEDGE
Andropogon virginicus

8-12 OZ (250-360G) BROWNISH PINK HEADS OF REEDS *OR* LEAVES AND STALKS OF BROOMSEDGE PICKED YOUNG AND GREEN, CHOPPED OR BRUISED

Reeds have a stout creeping underground stem and slender spikelet leaves. They grow 2 to 3 feet high and are found in damp places. The florets are short tufts of silky red-brown hair. Broomsedge is a common wayside grass about 2 to 3 feet tall with narrow pointed leaves breaking from high on the stem. The flowers are erect feathery tufts. Both reeds and broomsedge also dye wool yellow with alum mordant and a brass color with chrome mordant.

Mordant: Alum-soda or alum-tannin-alum gives yellows.

Method: Put the pieces in cold water and heat slowly. Simmer for 2 hours. Strain off the plant material and enter the clean, wetted cotton. Bring the bath to just under the boiling point and keep at this temperature for ½ to 1 hour. Rinse the cotton and dry.

WELD
Reseda luteola

3-6 OZ (90-180G) WHOLE PLANTS EXCEPT ROOTS, FRESH OR DRIED, ROUGHLY CHOPPED

¼ OZ (7G) OR 1½ TBSP POWDERED CHALK

1 OZ (30G) OR A SCANT TBSP CRUSHED COPPER SULFATE

See page 45 for a description of weld and the recipe for dyeing wool. It is also a good dye for silk, which is mordanted and treated in the same way as wool. Pick weld in summer before it seeds.

Mordant: Alum-tannin-alum gives yellow.

Method: Put the pieces in cold water and heat slowly. Simmer for up to 3 hours. Strain off the plant material and stir in the chalk and copper sulfate. Enter the clean, wetted cotton and bring bath to just under the boiling point. Keep at this temperature for ½ to 1½ hours. Rinse the cotton and dry.

MARIGOLD

Tagetes species

See page 49 for a description of the marigold and the recipe for dyeing wool.

Mordant: Alum-tannin-alum gives yellow.

Method: Put the flower heads in cold water and heat slowly. Simmer for 10 to 15 minutes. Strain off the heads and enter the clean, wetted cotton. Bring the bath to just under the boiling point and keep at this temperature for 20 to 30 minutes. Rinse the cotton and dry.

1-2 GALS FRESHLY PICKED FLOWER HEADS OR ½ THIS QUANTITY DRIED FLOWER HEADS

COTTON FLOWERS

Gossypium species

This is the plant from which cotton fibers are produced. It is too well known in the regions where it grows to merit description here. It also dyes wool, producing a bright orange-yellow without a mordant.

Mordant: Alum-tannin-alum gives yellow.

Method: Steep the cotton flowers in the water to be used for dyeing for 15 to 20 minutes, strain, and enter the clean, wetted cotton. Bring bath to just under the boiling point and keep at this temperature for ½ hour. For a tan color, enter the cotton in a hot afterbath of vinegar and chrome and simmer for 10 to 15 minutes. Keep afterbath covered. Rinse the cotton and dry.

½ QT DRIED COTTON FLOWERS, CRUSHED LIGHTLY

AFTERBATH
1½ TBSP VINEGAR
AND
SCANT ½ TSP CHROME PER GAL OF WATER

Recipes for Autumn

1 QT AUTUMN BERRIES, GLOWING RED AND BRUISED

AFTERBATH

SCANT ½ TSP FERROUS SULFATE PER GAL OF WATER

SUMAC

Rhus species

See page 60 for a description of sumac and the recipe for dyeing wool.

Mordant: Alum-soda gives light yellow-tan, iron (afterbath) for gray.

Method: Put the berries in cold water and steep overnight in the water to be used for dyeing. Heat slowly and simmer for 2 hours. Strain off the berries and enter the clean, wetted cotton. Bring the bath to the simmer and simmer for 20 to 30 minutes, testing for the color — longer may spoil it. For a gray color, enter the cotton in a hot afterbath of iron and simmer for 10 to 15 minutes. Rinse the cotton and dry.

2 OZ (60G) OR 2/3 CUP DRIED BERRIES, CRUSHED, OR ¼ THIS QUANTITY OF EXTRACT

AFTERBATH
2 TBSP VINEGAR
AND
SCANT ½ TSP CHROME PER GAL OF WATER

BUCKTHORN

Rhamnus caroliniana and R. cathartica

See page 71 for a description of buckhorn and the recipe for dyeing wool. Buckthorn extract is available from dye houses and some drug suppliers.

Mordant: Alum-tannin-alum with chrome after bath gives warm yellow to tan.

Method: If berries are used, put them in cold water, heat slowly, simmer for ½ hour, and strain; if extract is used, stir it into the bath and enter the clean, wetted cotton. Bring the bath to just under the boiling point and keep at this temperature for 20 to 40 minutes. Then enter the cotton in a hot afterbath of vinegar and chrome and simmer, covered, for 10 to 15 minutes. Rinse the cotton and dry.

BUTTERNUT

Juglans cinerea

This 80-foot-high tree of North America has twigs of a purplish brown and lanceolate leaves. The fruit is large and sticky and the nut is prominently ridged. Butternut also dyes wool with an alum mordant.

Mordant: Alum-tannin-alum gives brown to green, iron gives a good gray.

2 QTS GREEN BUTTERNUT HULLS

AFTERBATH

SCANT ½ TSP FERROUS SULFATE PER GAL OF WATER

Method: Steep the hulls in the water to be used for dyeing for ½ hour and then heat slowly. Simmer for 30 minutes. Strain off the hulls and enter the clean, wetted cotton. Bring the bath to just under the boiling point and keep at this temperature for about 30 minutes. This will give a color from brown to green, depending on the condition of the hulls. For gray, enter the cotton in a hot afterbath of iron and simmer for 10 to 20 minutes. Rinse the cotton and dry.

Recipes for Winter

BLACK OAK
Quercus velutina

RED OAK
Quercus borealis

HICKORY
Carya tomentosa

WESTERN HEMLOCK
Tsuga heterophylla

All these trees are described in Chapter 3, and recipes for dyeing wool are given.

Mordant: Alum-tannin-alum gives gold with black oak, rose-tan with red oak, gold to orange with hickory and rose-tan with western hemlock.

Method: Steep the bark overnight or longer in the water to be used for dyeing. Heat slowly and simmer for 2 hours. Strain off the bark and enter the clean, wetted cotton. Bring the bath to just under the boiling point and keep at this temperature for ½ to 1 hour. To bring out the color with red oak, chittam, and western hemlock, enter the cotton in a hot afterbath of vinegar and chrome and simmer, covered, for 10 minutes. Rinse the cotton and dry.

1 QT BARK, CHOPPED

AFTERBATH (FOR RED OAK AND WESTERN HEMLOCK)
2 TBSP VINEGAR
AND
SCANT ½ TSP CHROME PER GAL OF WATER

ONION SKINS
Allium cepa

See page 23 for the recipe for dyeing wool. Onion skins do not give the quick and dramatic effects with cotton that they produce with wool, but they provide a useful dye.

Mordant: Alum-tannin-alum gives yellow.

Method: Put the onion skins in cold water and heat slowly. Simmer for 1 hour. Strain off the oinon skins and enter the clean, wetted cotton. If the cotton has not been premordanted, stir in the alum and oak gall before entering the cotton. Bring the bath to just under the boiling point and keep at this temperature for up to 1 hour. This gives a soft yellow. By using three times the quantity of alum and three or four oak galls, I get shades from yellow-green through to a soft olive (the stickiness that too much alum gives to wool is much less noticeable with cotton). To deepen the colors, add the iron to the bath for the last 15 minutes of dyeing.Rinse the cotton and dry.

½-1 OZ (15-30G) OR A LARGE HANDFUL ONION SKINS, CRUSHED

1¾ TBSP ALUM
AND
1 OAK GALL, GROUND (IF COTTON IS NOT PREMORDANTED)

A PINCH OF FERROUS SULFATE (OPTIONAL)

MADDER

Rubia tinctorum

See pages 74-78 for a description of madder and the recipes for dyeing wool.

Mordant: Alum-tannin-alum gives dark red.

Cotton dyeing is done with successive baths, so the given quantities must be multiplied several times, depending on the depth of color desired.

½-1 oz (15-30ɢ) or 1½-1¾ ᴛʙsᴘ ᴄᴏᴍᴍᴇʀᴄɪᴀʟʟʏ ᴘʀᴏᴅᴜᴄᴇᴅ ᴍᴀᴅᴅᴇʀ ᴘᴏᴡᴅᴇʀ ᴏʀ ᴀᴛ ʟᴇᴀsᴛ 3 ᴛɪᴍᴇs ᴛʜɪs ᴀᴍᴏᴜɴᴛ ᴏғ ᴄʜᴏᴘᴘᴇᴅ ʀᴏᴏᴛs

1 ɢᴀʟ *ʜᴀʀᴅ* ᴡᴀᴛᴇʀ

¼ ᴛsᴘ ᴡᴀsʜɪɴɢ sᴏᴅᴀ (ᴏᴘᴛɪᴏɴᴀʟ)

Method: If you are using powder, add it to the water and stir; if you use roots, put them in a mesh bag and enter together with the clean, wetted cotton. Slowly bring the bath to hand-heat, about 90°-100°F. (32°-38°C.) and keep at this temperature for 1 hour. Leave the cotton to cool in the bath overnight. Adding the washing soda, dissolved in a little boiling water, just before the bath has begun to cool, will help the color to develop. To obtain a darker color repeat the procedure with a new infusion of madder. When the desired depth of color has been obtained, rinse the cotton and dry.

FUSTIC

Chlorophora tinctoria

OSAGE-ORANGE

Maclura pomifera

CUTCH

Acacia species

See page 86 for a description of fustic and the recipe for dyeing wool.

Osage-orange is a shrubby American tree belonging to the mulberry family. The spicy branches bear broad, lanceolate entire leaves. The flowers are greenish in round clusters, and the fruit is a round, yellowish green apple shape. Osage-orange is also known as bow-wood. This is a plant I have not had the opportunity to try myself, but I have it on good authority from American dyers.

Cutch is the name applied to the dye-bearing parts of two tropical trees, the Bengali *Acacia catechu,* whose dye resides in the colored heartwood and pods, and *Arica catechu,* the Asian palm that yields betel nuts.

Mordant: Alum-tannin-alum gives yellow with fustic and yellow-tan with osage orange. Cutch needs no mordant beforehand.

Method: If chips are used, put them in cold water, heat slowly, simmer for 20 minutes to 1 hour and strain off the chips. If cutch extract is used, stir it in and enter the clean, wetted cotton. Bring bath to just under the boiling point and keep at this temperature for 30 minutes. Enter in a hot afterbath of vinegar, chrome, and (if cutch is used) copper sulfate and simmer, covered, for 10 minutes. Rinse the cotton and dry.

½-1 OZ (15-30G) FUSTIC OR OSAGE-ORANGE CHIPS OR ¼ THIS AMOUNT OF CUTCH EXTRACT

AFTERBATH
2 TBSP VINEGAR
AND
SCANT ½ TSP CHROME PER GAL OF WATER

¼ TSP COPPER SULFATE (WITH CUTCH ONLY)

INDIGO

Indigofera tinctoria

Indigo is an excellent dye for cotton and has been used all over the world for this fiber. To dye cotton, follow the recipe on page 82. It does not need a mordant, but the color can be varied by mordanting with alum-soda or alum-tannin-alum.

SOME DYES FOR SILK

Silk is mordanted in the same way as wool, although a little more alum and a little less tin than used for wool are advisable. Iron is not used on silk. Silk must be well washed in hot soapy water before mordanting or dyeing. The dyeing process is the same as for wool, but about *double* the amount of dyestuff should be used because silk has less affinity for plant dyes and because the temperature must be kept a little lower — about 185°F. (85°C.) — to preserve the lustrous quality of the silk. Since silk is slower to take up the dye, it is also a good idea to leave it to steep in the dyebath for some hours or overnight after dyeing. Then it should be rinsed thoroughly and dried.

Of the historical dyes, cochineal, indigo, and kermes are all excellent for silk, and madder may also be used. Among the other plant dyes that are good silk dyes are turmeric, weld, marigold, barberry, and lily of the valley for yellow; black oak for orange; tobacco, pokeberry, and acorns for browns; sloe for rose-purple and elderberry and wild grape for purples; bracken and blackberry tips for gray; and logwood for black. Silk can be top-dyed too, so a combination of marigold and indigo, or cochineal and indigo, will give greens and purples.

6. Top-Dyeing

The colors available to the dyer from single plants, even considering the variety possible from different durations of dyeing and different mordants, are still far from evenly distributed over the spectrum. In most cases foliage dyes yellow to green, the majority of barks, yellow or brown to mushroom-pink. We get red from some roots, and various colors from flower heads. But by top-or double-dyeing, or over-dyeing, as it is sometimes called, a much greater variety can be obtained. Since dyeing one color over another always tends to dull the final color, it is best to use clear, bright colors for the first dye. Weld, madder, and indigo are all great standbys. It is usually better to dye the lighter color first.

When dyeing with any of the bright yellows, such as weld, fustic, buckthorn, or dyer's greenwood, I dye a number of extra skeins to keep for top-dyeing. The lemon-yellows of buckthorn, broom, and barberry and the greenish yellows of lily-of-the-valley, broomsedge, and heather, all mordanted with alum or tin, are the best bases to combine with blue for top-dyed greens. Dyer's greenwood was for many centuries top-dyed with woad to make greens. Nowadays usually indigo is used to get bright greens. (Since setting up an indigo vat just to top-dye for green or purple is a lot of trouble, when I have an indigo vat going I dye many different fibers and samples of cloth, so that I can have them ready to top-dye when occasion arises.) The warm yellows of onion skins, goldenrod, and marigold and the golds of black oak, ragwort, and weld, with chrome or alum mordants, are naturally better for orange to coral colors, and are often top-dyed with madder. Olive green which is a warm shade, would be made by dyeing blue over a warm yellow rather than a cool, acid yellow.

Black is one of the most difficult colors to obtain with plant dyes (yellow flag iris roots are the nearest I can get with one plant), so to make black I use cutch to top-dye the darkest blue I can obtain with repeated dips of indigo. Or I top-dye a dark blue from logwood chips with cutch mordanted with iron. If working only with the plants of my neighborhood, I dye the darkest brown I can get from rotten black walnut husks, with iron added at the end, and steep the wool in the liquor after dyeing; then I top-dye by dipping repeatedly in woad or by simmering in sloe or blackberry liquor. Afterward I wash the wool in a soapy solution to bring up the blue.

A few basic recipes are enough to suggest how, by top-dyeing, you can obtain certain colors stronger or faster than is possible with only one plant.

Whatever color you dye first, it is usually better to go straight on to the second after rinsing out the first, or to wrap the fiber in a towel overnight so that it remains damp. If, however, the skeins have been stored for some time as I suggested, then it is necessary to get them thoroughly wetted again by soaking them for some hours or even overnight in a bath of warm water. Then squeeze them (or put through a wringer at light pressure) and lay out for about ½ hour to let the remaining dampness spread evenly throughout the fibers. If even dyeing is important, this preparation is really necessary.

TO MAKE GREEN FROM INDIGO ON YELLOW

Use alum-mordanted wool previously dyed with weld, dyer's greenwood, snowberry, broom flowers, etc., or alum-tannin-mordanted cotton dyed with broomsedge, marigold or buckthorn.

Method: Dye the wetted yellow skeins in an indigo vat following the recipe on page 83 and hang in the air. Dip once or twice for a yellow-green, three to five times for a medium green, and many times for a dark blue-green. Rinse and dry.

It is also possible to dye the wool blue first, air, rinse thoroughly, and let the fullest blue that is going to develop with oxidation come through, and then simmer in a yellow bath. But I think it is easier to control the color by repeated dips of blue that show what kind of green is emerging.

TO MAKE ORANGE TO FLAME FROM MADDER ON YELLOW

Use alum-mordanted wool previously dyed with weld, dyer's greenwood, fustic, black oak, etc, or alum-tannin-mordanted cotton dyed with broomsedge, marigold, turmeric, or weld.

Method: To a gallon of *hard* water (or soft water to which 3 teaspoons of powdered chalk has been added), add 1½ tablespoons alum, 2 teaspoons cream of tartar, and 6 tablespoons madder extract. If possible, steep overnight. Heat to just over hand-heat. Enter the clean, wetted yellow fiber, and bring the bath slowly to the simmer. (It does not matter if the bath gets too hot in this case, since you are aiming at orange, and madder yields *yellows* at higher temperatures, but simmering should be enough to produce a firm dye.) According to the depth of orange required, simmer the wool for 10, 20 or 30 minutes. Rinse and dry. Remember that the first yellow is fixed, but some of the madder red will wash out in the rinsing.

TO MAKE PURPLE FROM COCHINEAL ON BLUE

Use wool previously dyed blue with indigo or woad. You can top-dye chrome-mordanted wool with madder, but cochineal gives a clear, pinker red.

Method: To a gallon of soft water, add 2 tablespoons cochineal (pounded in a mortar or steeped in a little water for some hours beforehand), ½ teaspoon common salt, a scant ½ teaspoon stannous chloride, and 2 teaspoons cream of tartar, and heat slowly. Simmer for up to 15 minutes. Enter the clean, wetted blue fiber and simmer until the desired depth of color is reached. Rinse and dry. Remember that some of the red will rinse out, but if the fiber is a blue-purple when dried, it may be entered again for a second simmering.

7. Lichen Dyes

Lichens are a very unusual kind of plant, composed of two different organisms — tiny blue-green algae (related to the common free-living algae) and colorless fungal threads. "These two components grow together in harmonious association referred to as symbiosis, or simply 'living together.' Lichen symbiosis, however, differs basically from all other kinds in that a new plant body, the thallus, is formed, and this thallus has no resemblance to either a fungus or an algae growing alone. This new composite organism behaves as a single independent."* Thus lichens differ from mosses, which have a rudimentary differentiation into stems and leaves and are green because they make chlorophyll.

Lichens grow in many different parts of the world, in all temperatures and at most altitudes. They grow on the ground, by the seashore, on trees (where it is difficult to separate them from the bark), on rocks and houses and roofing tiles. But above all they grow in the tundra regions and on the mountains, higher than any other plants. Whereas trees did not grow above 13,500 feet nor flowering plants above 18,000 feet, lichens were found on Mount Everest above 20,000 feet. This means that they serve a most important purpose in clothing the earth. In the tundra of Lapland they support herds of reindeer, caribou, musk-ox, and moose, on which the Lapps live. Because the herds devour great quantities of lichen which grows very slowly, taking years to mature to fodder size, the herds have to travel over great areas to graze, and therefore the Lapps are forced to be nomadic people.**

*Mason Hale, *Know the Lichens*, 1969.

**In *People of the Deer*, Farley Mowat, who lived with them, gives a fascinating picture of this life.

There are thousands of species of lichens, and the dye properties of multitudes have probably not yet been discovered, but there are a few families well known as dye-plants from which the enthusiast can obtain a sure dye. Meanwhile one can experiment with any others that can be found.

The lichens have other interesting uses besides dyeing. In 1866 an archaeological investigation of prehistoric remains at Lake Constance in Switzerland found, far down below layers of peat, and among reindeer horns and bones, stores of lichen — probably in reserve for animal food. It is still used as human food by the Laplanders in times of scarcity, and has saved the lives of starving Arctic explorers. "Iceland moss" and "reindeer moss" — names given before the distinctive nature of lichens was understood — are dried, powdered, mixed with flour, and baked as bread or boiled with milk into a broth. The bitter taste arising from the very acids that make them valuable as a dye can in food be neutralized with soda.

In the arid lands of North Africa and the Near East occurs the manna lichen (*Lecanora esculenta*), which is blown down the mountain sides and collects inches deep in the valleys. It used to be thought that this was the "manna" of the Bible and it was named "Bread from Heaven," but this is no longer accepted.

Lichens have been used in tanning as well as in brewing, for the thallus will ferment in dilute acid. But this process could never be carried out on any great scale because once stripped from the neighborhood, lichens grow too slowly to make it economical.

Lichens have also been used in perfumery along with other plants because the thallus has the power of retaining scent. John Gerard's *Herbal* of 1597 mentions a moss that "is to be used in compositions which serve for sweet perfumes and that takes away wearisomeness." This was probably oak moss (*Evernia prunastri*). It was used in scented hair powders and is still used in potpourri, where layers of freshly gathered flowers and lichens are placed alternately. The flowers are renewed each day until the lichens are permeated with their distinctive scent — roses, carnations, or whatever.

Lichens were used as a medicine from very ancient times (some Iceland moss was found in an Egyptian tomb of the Eighteenth Dynasty) but with doubtful efficacy. But there is no question about the age-old value of lichen dyes. When the prophet Ezekiel said, "blue and purple from the isles of Elishah was that which covered thee," he may well have been referring to colors from lichens. Pliny the Elder wrote of "the crisp leaves used in Crete for dyeing garments," which was probably the lichen *Roccella*, for it had long been known in the Near East, and the Phoenicians used it. The Tyrian purple of the classical world, mentioned in Chapter 4, which was made from the *Murex* shellfish, was so precious that an extract of it was often dyed over the purple made from *Roccella*. Gradually the use of *Murex* died out, until the lichen alone provided the purple dye, and still does. *Roccella* flourished on the Mediterranean coasts, and new sources were found in the Canaries and Cape Verde Islands in the eighteenth century. When these sources declined in the following century, India and Ceylon supplied Britain, and the dye was imported into America ready for use. One American dyer, writing of lichens in 1869, spoke of the "peculiar softness and velvet bloom it communicates to colors." * Since the *Roccella* had to be imported at great expense from the Mediterranean shores or farther east, it came to be supplemented by Scandinavian lichens and lichens indigenous to the United States, gathered by country people and dispatched to dye centers.

The first synthetic chemical dye, produced in Germany in the mid-nineteenth century, was a strong purple — in contrast to the soft muted colors of the lichen and other natural dyes. The quality of the color is of course one way of dating textiles of this period; the harsh brightness of the new dye, which was taken up with indiscriminate enthusiasm, strikes an alien note. Unlike the earlier synthetics, plant dyes seem to grow together as they fade over the centuries.

In Scotland and Ireland lichen dyeing was extensively used and has continued to be, especially in the cottage industries. No one knows how long the remote highland and island dwellers have had this knowledge — possibly since the Bronze Age settlers brought their metal-craft and their distinctive Celtic forms of decoration to Ireland and Scotland. The Scottish tartans were dyed with lichens, and they were so colorful that they were a disadvantage to the clansmen on the hills; most families had a more somber "hunting tartan" in addition. In the kilts and plaids of these times still extant, the old colors have faded but they have faded consistently and together produce a mellow effect. Now a new range of these shades, more subtle than the late-nineteenth century synthetic tartan colors, is being manufactured under the name of "the ancient colors," and very beautiful they are.

The highland tweed industry used lichen and seaweed dyes until recently, and the distinctive smell of them lingers for years. As a child I had an orange-pink Harris tweed wool coat of a color that I never saw again until I got it by experimenting myself. All this knowledge was handed on for centuries by word of mouth and there were very few written references before our generation.**

The use of lichen dyes is known to the Indians of the southwest United States and we have a record of Navajos boiling the *Parmelia molluscula* with natural alum to get orange, and leaving it in the dyebath overnight to get a reddish tan. Juniper ashes were used as an alternative mordant.

Because they are widespread over the globe, because they can be dried and used in winter, and because they do not need a mordant, lichens offer a rich source to the plant dyer and entice us to explore a field where there is still a great deal of original discovery to be made.

GENERAL NOTES ON COLLECTING LICHENS

All lichens grow rather slowly, many taking fifty to a hundred years to reach the size of a hand, so all but the commonest should be gathered without waste. Some are so rare that they should not be wantonly removed. They all swell in the rain and so are easier to gather in damp weather, and they are commoner and

*Quoted by Rita Adrosko in *Natural Dyes in the United States,* 1968.

**Among these references are Dr. Lauder Lindsey's "On the Dyeing Properties of Lichens," Edinburgh, 1855, and the articles on Archil Dyes and Lichens in the Encyclopaedia Britannica, 1798.

more various in the damp west of Britain — Cornwall, Wales, the Lakes, and Scotland, especially where there are exposed rocks. They flourish in the humid atmosphere of the tropics; in arid places they rely on the heavy dew and grow less large. They all need light and clean air — they will not survive near smoky cities, and are in fact used as a test of air pollution.The so-called crustaceous lichens form a crust on rocks or tree barks, and are best gathered in May and June — after rain if possible. The "foliaceous" lichens expand outwards in leafy lobes and are best gathered in early autumn after the summer heat has produced the greatest concentration of acids. But it is possible to gather lichens at any time of year if you avoid the dry, windy days when the powdery dust would be lost. Scrape the lichens off with a sharp knife and gather them directly into bags closed with a rubber band. Spread them to dry thoroughly in the sun, in an airing cupboard, or even in a warm oven, up to 200°F. (93°C.) If they are to be kept without going moldy, they are best hung in nylon-stocking bags in a dry place.

In the old days children were taught by the family to identify the dye lichens by sight as surely as we do vegetables today. The many thousands of lichens are hard to describe verbally sufficiently clearly to make identification sure, so I will give only the briefest description of a few main ones. Eileen Bolton's excellent book, *Lichens for Vegetable Dyeing,* has color pictures and enlargements. But the best method is to make a quick test of a little bit of every lichen you find by simmering it with a skein of wool in an enamel mug or ovenproof glass, and to keep some of the lichen itself dried with the dyed wool.

GENERAL PRINCIPLES FOR DYEING WITH LICHENS

As a rough guide, use 4 ounces (120 grams) of lichen to 4 ounces of wool for testing; however, many lichens have a great amount of dye potential and you will need much less: only an ounce or less of many that are fermented with ammonia (as described below).

Since the dye acids may lie under the skin of the plant or right in the center, it is very important to bruise the *fresh* plants well between the hands or shred with kitchen scissors, and to crumble the *dry* lichens, breaking across the whole center.

The powdery and coral-like growths on the surface may contain dye, so it is better not to wash lichens. Dust and small insects will not affect the dye but tannin will, so pick out scraps of bark. Lichens swell in water, and you must allow for this in the size of the dyebath, but many lichens are better soaked the night before and boiled up in the same water. Water from streams that have run through peat bogs are better for lichen dyes than water that is artificially softened. I have tried soaking a bit of peat in a pail of rainwater to use in my hard-water district.

Without going into the complexities of the thousands of lichen species and the different acids that affect the color (the same lichens may develop different acids in different continents), the amateur dyer can put lichens in four categories:
   1) Lichens that yield their dye with boiling only.
   2) Lichens that yield their dye with fermentation with ammonia.

The process of steeping lichens in some form of ammonia is referred to as "maceration," and lichens like the *Roccellas* yield in this way a dye-producing substance called archil, orchil, or cudbear, which can be isolated and dried. This extract can be obtained from some dyehouses.

3) Lichens that yield different colors from the two methods.

4) Lichens that yield no dye by any known method.

There is a simple test by which to know if a lichen will yield its dye by fermentation.* The presence of two of the acids that yield a deep red or purple dye when fermented in ammonia can be detected by a simple household bleach containing chlorine (calcium hypochlorite) or caustic lye (potassium hydroxide). It *is* caustic, so handle it with care. The chlorine bleach is abbreviated "Cl" here, since chlorine is the active agent, and the lye is shortened to the common "KOH."

These chemicals react on the thallus, so you must scrape away the outer skin of the lichen with a sharp knife, until a small spot of the white under-layer is exposed.

Apply a drop of Cl or KOH to this spot — an eyedropper is convenient. If the exposed surface turns red, this lichen will yield to fermentation. If neither Cl or KOH produce this reaction, then try boiling. A quick way to establish whether a lichen will yield a dye is the contact method of boiling, described below.

Lichens dye well on wools and silk, and one at least — dog's tooth lichen — dyes cotton and linen.

The lichens do not require mordants, but interesting variations of color can be obtained by adding different substances — all the basic mordants, alum, chrome, tin, iron, and also copper sulfate, ammonium sulfate, tannic acid. There is still much to be explored.

Boiling Water Methods Of Dyeing With Lichens

Contact Method: A traditional Scottish method that I have often used is to pack alternate layers of lichen and wool in the vessel, cover with soft water, and simmer for up to 3 hours, watching to see the water does not evaporate and topping up with boiling water. Here the dye is accepted by direct contact.

Quick Liquor Method: A more usual method is to put the lichens in soft water (if they have been dried they should soak overnight in the water), preferably with 2 tablespoons vinegar to each gallon water. Bring slowly to boiling point and simmer for 3 hours. I generally save time by putting the wetted wool in at the start, but many dyers prefer to cool the bath down and put in the wool the next day, and then slowly raise the temperature. Since lichen colors do not wash out much, the color can be judged well when wet, and the bath is continued until you reach the required color. You can take out samples at 10 minutes, 20 minutes, and so on for comparison.

If the dye is slow to "run" from the plants, you can add a few drops of

---

*I owe my knowledge of this test to Marie Aitken of Ontario, Canada, who has used lichens in the Arctic.

ammonia to the bath; if this is not enough, try 2 or 3 teaspoonfuls. Many of the purples are improved by adding washing soda to the dyebath. Casutic soda (which unfortunately makes the wool brittle) also excites the color to flow.

Traditional Liquor Method: The lengthier method is to put up to 4 ounces (120 grams) of the lichen in 1 gallon of soft water to which a tablespoon of vinegar has been added to make it acid. Bring this to the boiling point slowly — it should take nearly an hour — and then keep it simmering for 3 hours longer. Allow it to cool slowly, possibly overnight. Enter the wetted wool, and bring the whole to simmering point again for an hour or longer, according to the strength of color. During this time move the wool around gently from time to time. Leaving it in the bath to cool will produce a firmer but deeper color. After this rinse it, and when it is dry, shake to remove the scraps of lichen in it.

The dye lichens are colloquially known as "crottles" or "crottals" in Scotland and Ireland. Their common names and scientific names are given here.

The following lichens yield dye by boiling.

PARMELIA CAPERATA

A pale yellowish-green leathery lichen, black underneath (except at the edges), found on rocks or barks, this is known as green stone lichen, stone crottal, or arcel. It is quite common in the damper parts of Britain and in the United States, especially on sandstone and on oak trees. It yields a good yellow with boiling. Leaving in pieces of oak bark will give a brownish yellow.

Two other parmelias, *P. furfuracer* and *P. perlata,* give better results when fermented.

PARMELIA SAXATILIS

Common names of this widely distributed gray plant are gray stone crottal, stoneyraw, or scrottyie. It has an ashy powder effect on top and black underneath with short black hairs, and grows outward in frilly lobes. It is found mostly on rocks and stones in Britain and Scandinavia and is also common on oak and pine trees in the United States. It is a dye of long standing in all these countries, widely used for fine bronze color that is typical of Harris tweeds and gives them a distinctive smell.

PARMELIA OMPHALODES

This dark purplish brown lichen, known as black crottal, crostil or arcel, spreads in flat cushions over rocks at higher altitudes than the other parmelias, in Britain, Scandinavia, and the United States. The underside is very black with close black hairs. Boiling gives a fine strong red-brown with excellent fastness. It too has the characteristic smell of Harris tweed, for which it was extensively used.

LOBARIA PULMONARIA

A large foliacious lichen usually on trees, especially oak, dark olive when wet and almost brown when dry. The underside is downy and ochre-colored. Known as lungwort or hazel crottal, it is common in Scandinavia, Britain, and temperate regions of the United States, especially the Great Lakes and Pacific West, where the high forests shelter it. It takes a very long time to grow and should be harvested with great care. It makes a good brown dye, which was used by Hereford farmworkers to dye their stockings.

HYPOGYMNIA PSYCHODES
Previously known as *Parmelia physodes*

This common lichen of rocks and trees, known as shield lichen or dark crottal, has a wrinkled, swollen-looking thallus, gray on top and dark brown underneath. At the lobe ends are pimples of fruits which produce a white powder. This lichen hangs so tenuously that it often falls off. It is common in woods and on cut wood structures and also on rocks in the mountain regions of Britain, Scandinavia, and the United States, especially the damp Northwest. It gives a good golden brown.

PELTIGERA CANINA

This lichen is known as dog's tooth lichen or ash-colored ground liverwort. Large overlapping lobes of dark greenish brown, which turn ashen and papery on drying, characterize this lichen. It often grows on old wood stumps, and among mosses and grass on the ground.

This lichen will dye linen yellow with an alum mordant when boiled for 30 minutes.

Another of the *Peltigera* species of America is said to give a rose-tan on wool with ¼ teaspoon chrome and 2 teaspoons vinegar. Other *Peltigeras* can be fermented.

Fermentation Method Of Dyeing With Lichens

Those lichens that give a positive reaction to the test with Cl or KOH may be treated in this way. As with the boiling method, crumble or cut fresh plants well with scissors, and break up dry plants finely by crumbling them in the hands. Put the pieces in a dish with a close fitting lid (I use glass jam jars with screw tops but wide pyrex glass dishes might be easier). Pour over them a mixture of 1 part ammonia to 2 parts soft water. (Some lichens will respond better to equal parts water and ammonia, but the 1-to-2 mixture is a good general rule.) The liquid should just cover the lichens adequately and may have to be topped up if the mass swells. Close the container and keep it in a light, even sunny, warm place (between 55° and 75°F. or 13° and 24°C.). Keeping the container tightly closed is important, or the ammonia will escape. Yet the mixture must be aerated frequently if the lichen is to ferment well; you should stir it a minimum of twice a day and much more frequently if possible, replacing the lid at once. This is a nuisance but it does yield some wonderful dyes. (I believe that an aeration pump for a fish tank might be the answer but I have not got further than using a bicycle pump jammed in a short glass tube.) The dye will begin to run, probably in a few days, and with, say, the cudbear lichen or rock tripe, you can get a fine soft purple after 10 days to 2 weeks. The addition of a little washing soda to the dyebath will turn this towards a blue purple, and vinegar or acetic acid towards a red. However, the mass of fermenting material can be left for many weeks yet to obtain a strong dark color.

When the color is running well, you can boil the whole fermenting mass of lichen and liquor, covered lightly, into a gelatinous liquor which can be used immediately (add enough water to give the fiber room to move freely) in the normal dyebath routine. It can also be stored, again with the lid on, or you can allow it to dry out and keep the powder.

The following lichens yield dye by fermentation.

UMBILICARIA PUSTULATA

This swollen, circular, single thallus called rock tripe is attached to the surface of rocks by a single stout "navel cord" (hence its Latin name). It is dark shiny green when wet, and when dry, velvety gray and dark brown. It grows sparsely in Britain and mostly in altitudes over 1,000 feet in the United States, but it is commoner in the tundra regions. It dries well but must be kept completely dry. It repays long maceration — up to years — in ammonia. It yields a strong bright red when fermented.

OCHROLECHIA PARELLA
Previously known as *Lecanora parella*

The curious appearance of its protruding fruits gave this plant its name: crawfish lichen, crab's eye, or light crottal. It is a greenish gray, whitish underneath, and crusty in its growth on stones, stone walls, and damp rocks. It was historically important: called *Orseille d'Auverne,* a variation of archil, it was gathered in the north of England for the London archil-makers. It was long used in the highlands of Scotland fermented with urine for the traditional orange-red of many tartans. It also occurs in Scandinavia and the United States.

OCHROLECHIA TARTAREA
Previously known as *Lecanora tartarea*

This thick, crustaceous thallus, cudbear lichen or korkir, which has been described as resembling a small cauliflower head, is whitish gray with flesh-colored spots and grows on rocks in Britain, Scandinavia, and parts of the United States. The traditional Scottish and Welsh crofters dried this lichen, powdered it into urine, and after many weeks made it up into balls with lime or

powdered shells, which were hung up to dry. When required it was boiled up with some alum and made a strong dark red.

My method is to crumble the lichens into a glass or plastic container with a lid and ferment it as described. After a few days, when it is producing a good red color, I boil it with the wool, and it produces a fine red-purple. It can be kept for some time in firmly screw-topped jars, or it can be evaporated in a warm place and the resulting powder stored dry. If a little washing soda is added when you boil it, it will turn towards blue-purple; the addition of a few teaspoons of acetic acid (or 4 tablespoons of vinegar) will bring out the redness. It is a very strong dye if properly prepared, and less than 1 ounce (30 grams) will dye four times that amount of wool.

CLADONIA IMPEXA

This fine gray lichen with much-divided hairlike branches grows among moss and heather in Cornwall and west European countries and in similar locations in the United States. It needs a long maceration to produce its soft pink dye.

ROCCELLA TINCTORIA

This first of the archil-producing lichens to be exploited is a Mediterranean species but it is also found in the Channel Islands near the sea, and dyers will want to use it for its historical interest.

The following lichens yield dye either by boiling or by fermenting.

XANTHORIA PARIETINA

This common plant, yellow wall lichen, is found on walls especially around farm buildings, on rocks just above high-water mark, and in all the shore areas of the United States, for it likes a salty atmosphere. Its bright orange-yellow glows in the sun; growing in the shade, it is rather greenish-blue. The thallus may be several inches across and has orange spots on the upper surface, while the under surface is whitish.

It gives a fine yellow dye, tending towards tan with boiling. When it is boiled after fermentation, with some soda added to the bath, a deep purple red is obtained. I followed Miss Bolton's method* and also got a fine blue from this red. Leave the wool in the dyebath after simple boiling and allow it to stand in a warm place until it is going "off" and smells a little. Then, on a bright sunny day gently squeeze out the wool and put it in the sun, where it will turn quite a bright blue; this blue fades a little at first but then retains its final color.

*See Eileen Bolton, *Lichens for Vegetable Dyeing*, 1960.

MENEGUSSIA PERTUSA

This pale greenish gray, much-frilled lichen grows on stones in Britain. With simple boiling it yields a yellow, which is improved by the addition of a little soda to the dyebath. After fermenting for a week it gives a fine soft pink, and if you increase the time, it will produce a deep reddish brown.

USNEA BARBATA

This tree moss, called beard lichen, is the "idle moss" mentioned by Shakespeare. Its gray-green hairs hang down a foot in length in Britain and more in the damp parts of the United States. It gives a clear yellow by simple boiling. Its relation *Usnea lirta* gives purple with fermentation.

EVERNIA PRUNASTRI

This plant, called stag's horn, bucks horn, ragged hoary lichen, or oak moss, has strap-shaped fronds, which first stand erect, then droop, not unlike stag's horns, and have an unpleasant limey smell. It is greenish gray above and white below, and grows on trees, old wood especially (hence the plum-tree of its Latin name) all over Britain and the temperate zones of the Unites States. It grows on a field-maple stump in my garden. Boiled, it gives a good brown; with fermentation, a beautiful plum purple.

As you can see, the lichens produce an extraordinary range of color. Anyone can begin lichen dyeing anywhere, with almost no equipment, and since lichens can be dried or stored after fermentation or boiling, this study can be carried over the whole year, even in arctic climates. There is still a great deal to be discovered, and a beginner who keeps careful records can both have the fun of making new colors and adding to our knowledge.

8. Using Dyed Fiber

When you have accumulated a number of dyed fibers, there are many interesting uses for them. Many dyers have some knowledge of stitchery, and those who have not can consult books with clear diagrams of stitches if there is no opportunity to attend a class. Dyeing has always been closely associated with weaving, and simple experimental weaving can be done with almost no equipment, combining wool and cotton with such fibers as raffia and rushes. (To obtain very thick fiber for bulky stitcheries or for rugs — woven, knotted, or crocheted — wash old garments in hot water to felt the fiber and prevent unraveling. Then cut them into strips ½ to 1 inch wide or into one continuous strip *parallel* to the line of the knitting or weave, and use these strips as though they were single strands.) A number of uses for the small quantities of yarn obtained from dye experiments are suggested in this chapter. More experienced dyers will doubtless wish to plan their work beforehand and to dye the quantities needed.

STITCHERY

By stitchery, I mean not only decorative embroidery but also the joining of pieces of cloth to make a shaped garment, cover, or container. We can still see in the costumes of peasant women in the remoter parts of Greece and Yugoslavia how the seams themselves may be decoratively stitched. With heavy cloth, it is often preferable to use an embroidery stitch such as herringbone or faggoting than to "sew and fell" with the triple thickness of cloth which that entails. The hem and sleeve edges of dresses made this way are often weighted and stiffened with many rows of stitchery, which gives a longer life to the garment. Another practical use of stitchery is to pleat or gather for fullness, and especially to gather in a way that allows elasticity, as in smocking. This is obviously invaluable for rapidly growing babies and for active people who need freedom in using their chest and shoulder muscles.

Stitchery may be used, as in appliqué, to make pictures to give visual pleasure, and we have many fine examples, all in vegetable dyes of course, from the middle ages to the Victorian era. Stitchery has been used, instead of pen or graver, to record, and here writing is often incorporated in the work, as with the Bayeux Tapestry. It has been used symbolically, as in the aprons and headdresses of certain Macedonian peasant wives, which have a form of decoration different from those in the unmarried girls. Throughout the centuries of the Christian church, stoles and copes have been embroidered with sacred symbols in traditional positions, and these are an essential part of ritual. This form of stitchery has had a vigorous revival today; embroiderers — both men and women — are making rich robes and altar frontals, footstools and cushions in contemporary styles. This work has traditionally been a labor of devotion for the Church, but these furnishings also offer a field for the needleworker in the home today.

A simple and fascinating form of stitchery suitable for filling odd hours and light to carry about is patchwork. Used blankets or white woven garments in wool or cotton can be cut up into regular shapes — perhaps four inch squares, or six-by-four rectangles — and two or four or more dropped into any bath where there is room to spare. They can then be assembled according to some plan or design and stitched up either simply by machine or by some decorative stitch such as herringbone or feather stitch. It usually proves necessary to have some color repeated throughout to hold the design together. A beautiful quilt was made in separate stuffed squares with their edges turned inwards, and oversewn. On the other hand, one of my students dyed and sewed together irregular rectangles in yellow, gold, soft greens and purples to make a cape. Another dyed small scraps of velvet for a square cushion and embroidered some of the squares with her dyed wool, achieving a rich effect from waste pieces.

The background material for stitchery — always of importance — is of prime consideration when vegetable-dyed fibers are used, especially if much of it is to show. Since many of the colors obtained from common wayside plants are in the brown and yellow-green ranges, the natural colors of unbleached wool, cotton, and linen provide a sympathetic background. In fact, for quick effects without strain on the eyes, sacking or burlap is a suitable background that costs nothing. Its natural jute color serves well, but jute can also be dyed by some plant dyes, such as indigo.

Almost all stitchery will be done on woven material, so the weave is an essential part of the whole. The coarser the weave, the more its structure obtrudes and must be incorporated in the whole.

The design on the cushion shown on page 118 shows a dyer's first effort with an extremely simple design inspired by a flower head and not drawn out beforehand. The background is walnut-brown burlap (hessian). The yellow wools were dyed with ragwort and tansy flowers, and the tufts of unspun natural fleece were stitched down. The fringed edge emphasizes the coarseness of the background material in a natural way, more appropriate here than finishing with a silk cord or a flounce.

There has been a great upsurge of interest in stitchery during recent years. Both men and women embroider free hangings, pictures to frame, and furnishings as well as clothes. Much of this is bold, colorful, and very free in style, using mixtures of fabrics, a variety of threads, and often incorporating natural objects such as shells, or pieces of metal. Many people are less inhibited by the idea of doing a piece of stitchery than making a painting, but they are doing expressive work similar to the artist's.

Since the first experiments in dyeing will probably result in short lengths of fiber, and it is difficult to know how much will be used up by a certain stitch, it is obviously unwise to start on an elaborate symmetrical design — you may not have enough of one color to finish it.

For the beginner in stitchery it is a good idea to learn one stitch, perhaps knot-stitch or featherstitch, to start, and try it in different thicknesses of thread and different spacings along the lines of the weave, which will serve as guiding lines and aid in keeping the size of the stitches equal. An interesting sampler can be made of a collection of vegetable dyes from a particular area or season by using the different threads in turn in this way. This also gives the opportunity to use up very short lengths from dye experiments. Later, the other possibilities of one stitch can be explored by seeing how it turns round corners, how it holds down a loose edge, or what is the effect of placing bands of it together in a solid mass.

One eight-year-old child in my classes made a sampler of stitches in different greens obtained from nettle on different fibers: cotton, tapes, ribbon, wool, and silk thread. A sampler need not be a laborious piece of work but may consist of short lengths—just enough to confirm that a stitch has been practiced sufficiently to become part of one's vocabulary.

Because cloth consists of threads woven at right angles, the beginner can give his work regularity by working in lines or squares or rectangles. Working with the weave also gives structure to the design without any intellectual "designing." But it is also fun to *play* with the structure of the cloth, to pull out threads, to vary the spacing, and perhaps to tie the parallel threads left in the space into some new arrangements. You can also make new combinations of color by pulling a dyed thread in — a good technique for heavy or nubbly dyed threads that cannot be put into the eye of a needle. First, pull out a number of warp threads (because these are bound to be strong enough to support the tug of the "pull through," whereas the weft may not be). Then, when there is enough room to maneuver, knot the new thread to one thread at the side of the gap and pull this thread through until the new thread lies in the position of the threads removed. If you want a bolder effect of the new color, remove the next warp threads — which follows a different path over and under — and lay a second thread of the new color next to the first. You can repeat this to get a band of any width. The effect need not be used over the total length of the cloth but can be limited to a shape within the whole if you simply cut the warp carefully between the weft threads: use a razor blade on cutting surface such as a kitchen chopping board.

Another variation is to cut the warp threads on one end only, hook them up a few inches back still attached at the other end, and leave them waving free like a fringe or stitch them down in another place, which adds to the textural quality. Here stitchery approaches closely some forms of contemporary weaving.

As I have suggested, the background material — unless it is canvas intended to be covered completely and even then the spacing determines the texture — is an important element in the final effect. But only a purist would suggest that its structure must always feature *obviously*. Some finely woven textiles serve admirably as background because of their plainness; with others that are already patterned, like Byzantine damasks, embroidery adds to the richness of the whole.

A tufted picture designed round the onion and other plants that provided the dyes is shown on page 119. It was completed during one weekend by a student fired with the excitement of seeing her own first dye colors emerge. In it several amounts of wool she had available — along with undyed wool — were cleverly used to show variety in the skin of the onion and the leaves. The curving edge echoes and complements the shapes within the picture, and shows the old-gold background of common burlap (hessian). This piece was thought of as a picture, but a similar work of soft tufted wool would make a comfortable cushion.

While the study of the leaf forms, calyxes, and fruits of plants themselves will provide many suggestions for designs and offer further outlets for expressing our interest in them, any subject is of course acceptable. But there is no need at all to design stitchery beforehand. Many fine contemporary embroideries have grown and taken form as they were made, and this approach is perhaps most fun of all. Simply start anywhere on the background — preferably near, but not dead-on, center — with one of the stronger colors, and stitch a shape, which need not represent anything but just an interesting shape! Then, changing the color and perhaps the thickness of the wool, add to that shape on one or several sides, building outwards from it in solid masses or in tenuous lines of stitchery, which can then be elaborated. They can spread asymmetrically to the edge, or new lines can be brought in from edge or corner to approach or perhaps mingle with them. Another way to begin a "free" embroidery is to use some pieces of dyed fabric — perhaps the background fabric dyed a different color or one that relates to it — cut and appliquéd on to provide the first solid patches of color. This gets a quicker effect and has an additional advantage: you can move the patches about before stitching them down to see where they look best in relation to the total shape. They can be of the same or different sizes, scattered or clustered, and their edges might be frayed and stitched down with small or decorative stitches between each thread. Since working *with* the nature of the material is one of the marks of the true craftsman, this underlining of the function of warp and weft can give great interest to such a stitchery.

Free embroidery has little formal design to hold it together, so it can lack unity unless the number of stitches is limited or the colors are repeated to some extent in different parts of the whole. Many vegetable-dye colors are apt to be very soft, and if too many of these "close-ranged" colors are used side by side, the effect will be misty and unclear, perhaps even confused. So it is wise to make clear steps from one shade to another and to have a dominant color or group of colors on which the eye can fasten, letting the others serve to enhance these. I know of no embroiderers working solely or mainly in plant-dyed colors in the western countries, so the time is ripe for those who wish to open up a new field.

WEAVING

Boundaries between many of the traditional crafts have almost been dissolved, and when we pull out threads of a material and weave in others with fingers or needle we are moving from stitchery into another craft, which gains its strength to survive by its own discipline and by the explorations of its highly skilled practitioners. But as an introduction to weaving, the beginner can use a cardboard loom, a simple frame of four pieces of wood screwed together, or an old picture frame. The spacing of the warp threads is controlled by knocking in tacks or nails at the required intervals on the two shorter bars. Start the warp at

Display of work inspired by American Indian weaving, pottery, and jewelry. At upper left is an Indian bow loom; at the right is a double bow loom. The fibers for the weaving and leather thongs for the jewelry were all dyed with plant dyes.

one end tack, and wind round the front and back of the frame, which gives you double the length of fabric you would have simply working on the front face. For a wall hanging you can hang the warp from a piece of natural wood and leave this in at the end. Or you can fasten one end of a long warp to a bar with a hook that can be slipped round a heavy chair or a tree branch and the other end to a bar fastened to your waistband, so that tension is created when you lean back. There are a number of excellent contemporary books on weaving (see the Bibliography), so I propose only to mention some points of special interest to the dyer.

Since the experimental dyer will probably be working mainly with wool, it should be noted that this fiber has bulk, softness, and an infinite range of colors, but its strength is not great, especially if it is a beginner's handspinning. So I strongly recommend setting up your first warp in cotton, linen, or a man-made fiber that has strength and just enough elasticity to make the shed — the path for the weft to go through. It is important to have firm selvedges, so use two or three threads in the place of one, or a heavier thread at the outside edges.

There is no reason why you should not from the beginning use threads of different thicknesses in the warp as well as in the weft. Small pieces of fancy-spun or unspun tufts can also be woven in with the weft. And once the beginning strip — about 1 or 1½ inches wide — is firmly in place, there is no reason why the weft should go all the way across. Interesting weavings can be built up (if they have not to stand up to hard usage) by weaving blocks and spaces, perhaps tieing the warp threads afterward in bunches.

There has been a tremendous explosion in the concept of weaving. We are surrounded by weaving as sculpture, three-dimensional and circular weaving, fascinating pouches and tubes that turn themselves inside out, garments woven in one piece, and so on, and these must make any new weaver feel that the field is very wide.

Dyers will naturally want to express their interest and pleasure in plants by incorporating some of them where appropriate in their weaving as well as in their stitchery. Birch bark can be fitted in the spaces between blocks of weft, and will curl round in an attractive fashion. Twigs and sprays with acorns, teasles, or tree fruits may be used in hangings, especially when they echo the dye materials used. Grasses create a beautiful texture, and their subtle colors often go well with soft dyed colors — a rush mat woven on a cotton warp dyed with rushes embodies the plant more fully than simply one or the other. Powdery or feathery heads like bullrushes (cattails) can be prevented from disintegrating by a thin coat of varnish. But I would plead against unusual additions simply for the sake of novelty or striking effect. The subtlety of plants demands sensitiveness in the worker. Also, while every weaving certainly does not need to have a practical purpose, directionless experiments (which clutter up the house flattered by the name of "wall hangings ") are just as pointless as the old rigid repetition. Experiments should be pieces from which we learn skills that can be incorporated in further, finer works. For instance, if one takes the trouble to learn the technique of gauze-weaving, which fastens down each weft throw, it is reasonable to vary the very open effects with all kinds of interesting objects — flower heads, leaf skeletons, even shells — as well as ceramic or metal pieces.

Hanging dyed completely with goldenrod, woven on a frame loom.

KNITTING AND CROCHET

The age-old crafts of knitting and crochet are of course the traditional techniques that relied on plant dyeing. Mittens of "sprang" (a technique similar to knitting) from the Bronze Age have been found in Danish bogs. The brightly colored knitted Scottish Fair Isle patterns use natural fleece along with dyes from seaweed and lichens, and have persisted for centuries. (The original abstract patterns, different from the Scandinavian representations of trees and animals so often found in Celtic art, may be Islamic patterns taught to the islanders by survivors of a Spanish galleon wrecked there as it fled from the Armada debacle.) Much of my own vegetable-dyed wool is made up in this form, not only because knitting is convenient to carry about, but also because I use up small scraps or skeins in such patterns.

The main thing to remember in knitting is that since wool threads spread a little and create misty rather than hard edges, it is necessary to use clearly defined colors, and the background and pattern should be different in *tone* —light colors on natural "black" sheep, or bright colors on white — otherwise, the effect will be fuzzy.

Crochet need not be the fine work done by our grandmothers for table linen or edging baby clothes. Crochet is very fashionable among young people, not only for clothing but also for three-dimensional pieces. You can use the results of dye experiments to make small single squares that can be sewn or crocheted together: it is also convenient if you always like to have a piece of handwork in one pocket for bus queues and airport waits. You can crochet with heavy wool made from twisting two or three threads together — if apparatus to ply professionally is not available — or with strips cut from old garments. I went to meet a woman who, I had heard, was teaching schoolchildren in Essex how to use woad (Essex used to have a considerable woad industry, so they were rediscovering their own history), and I found this delightful farmer's wife and a friend wearing their own dyed and woven tweed skirts and furnishing their houses with their own rugs. I remember in particular one circular floor rug crocheted in all the colors from dahlias, from dusky pink through orange to fawn and yellow.

KNOTTING AND PLAITING

The dyer's wool or cotton can also be used in some form of knotting, plaiting, tatting, or needle-weaving: these techniques make interesting forms that stand on their own or that can be used to hold objects such as fishermen's glass floats or even marbles by suspending them in a net. Uneven shapes can be held by cradling, a jewelry term for holding uncut semiprecious stones by bending wire around them. Acorns, decorative bean shapes, nuts, as well as shells, pebbles, and beads, may be incorporated.

Dyed fibers may also be made up in macramé. Macramé has been elaborated from old sailors' knots, and is now used to make a wide variety of functional and decorative forms, including large room dividers, window and door screens, as well as bags (either alone or combined with leatherwork). It is very suitable for

Crochet hanging, wool-bag, and scarf in natural and plant-dyed wools by students of the author.

this, being strong, light, and airy. My students have dyed macramé twine and cord with indigo when we had a vat set up, and with madder, walnut, and onion skins. Knotting and macramé can also be used to finish the warp ends of rugs, cushions, and hangings. In his book, *The Techniques of Weaving,* Peter Collingwood shows 29 different ways of finishing a fringe!

13
Patchwork cloak in wool cloth dyed with
summer plants of Pennsylvania, by a student
of the author.

14
Patchwork quilt made from over 500 separate
patches dyed with only four plants: raspberry,
sumac, indigo, and turmeric. The variety of
shades was obtained by the use of four
different mordants: iron, alum, chrome, and
tin, and by overdyeing. By a student of the
author.

15
Cushion with embroidery on the theme of the
umbel. By a student of the author.

16
Open weave dyed wool and string hanging by a
student of the author.

17
Woven hanging incorporating plants, by a
student of the author.

18
Tufted cushion with onion motif. The wool
was dyed with onion. By a student of the
author.

19
Punchwork (continuous thread stitchery) on
burlap by a student of the author. The fibers
were dyed with goldenrod, blackeyed susan,
blueberry, and sumac.

13

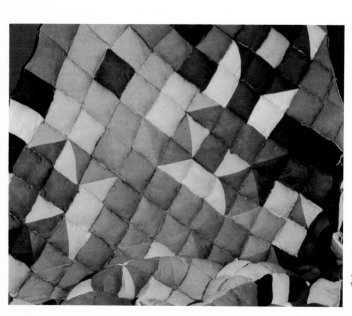

14

15

TIE-DYEING

The process of tie-dyeing, which is so useful for achieving quick and striking effects in banners, clothes, and furnishings, will be described only briefly here since there are excellent books on the subject. Tie-dyeing is usually done "in the piece," so the dyer is more likely to be working with cotton or silk than with woolen fabrics. Any of the appropriate plant dyes can be used, but much of the effect is lost if the dye is pale or indeterminate. So it is probably better to begin with one of the strong dyes — walnut, black oak, yellow flag iris roots, weld with iron mordant, or indigo, a longstanding favorite with the Nigerians, who still extensively practice tie-dyeing with indigo.

The simple theory is that if the dye is prevented from getting to certain parts of the cloth, these will remain white or the natural color, while the exposed parts will be colored and the parts between will show the fascinating path of the dye streaking along the fibers. This is the principle used in batik, where the areas not to be dyed are blocked out by pouring or brushing liquid wax over them. However, since almost all plant dyes require heating to near boiling point to be absorbed into the fiber, the wax would melt and expose the parts intended to be blocked out. Batik *is* used with the cool indigo vat, though, and dyers may want to experiment with it. In tie-dye, the areas not to be dyed are blocked out by binding the rolled or pleated cloth (or skeins of fiber) with string or by gathering it with a needle and strong thread so firmly that the dye cannot penetrate. Tieing and oversewing along the pleats can also be combined, as shown in the illustrations. It is necessary to pull up the string or thread very tightly, and to secure the ends firmly so the ties do not work loose.

The string or thread used must be very strong, and should have a waxy surface so the string itself will not absorb the dye and carry it into the covered parts. Since one does not always know how absorbent a string is, I usually begin

a *A handkerchief or piece of old cloth folded and ready for tieing.*
b *The handkerchief tied up with thread or thin string and thick twine wound around, and with thread wound spirally. All the ends are tied tightly and securely.*

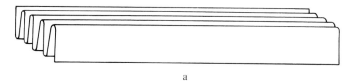

a

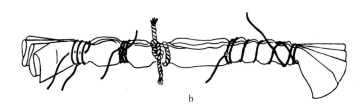

b

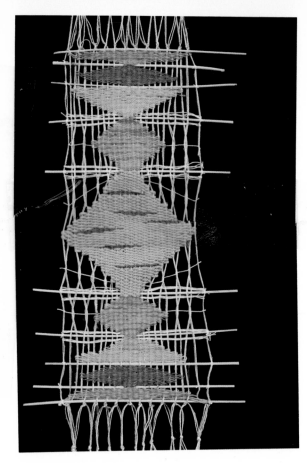

16

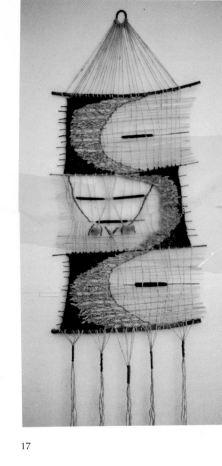

17

18

19

students with dyeing a piece of pleated cloth tied with all the threads, strings, and twines we can muster. As we untie, we can see which have best blocked the dye. Absorbent string can be painted over with flour and water paste, which cooks in the heat instead of melting as wax would. For this, blend 1 tablespoon flour or other thickening agent such as corn flour or cornstarch with a little water to a smooth paste, add to a cup of boiling water and cook 5 minutes.

Probably the easiest way to get the idea of tie-dyeing is to tie up three small experiments, for which you can use scraps of cotton cloth or cheap white handkerchiefs. Old cotton is very good for these experiments. As always before dyeing cotton, if it is new, it must be thoroughly washed.

1) In the center of one square, very accurately, put a smooth stone, a button, or a marble, and tie securely round. Put different shapes and sizes in each of the four corners and tie in the same way.

2) Fold the second square into even pleats 1 inch or less wide — ironing them in makes this easier — and tie at intervals down the length, trying one wide tie, two ties close together, a group of close ties with thick thread.

a *A handkerchief picked up by the exact center ready for tieing.*
b *The handkerchief with a bead or stone tied into it.*
c *The handkerchief with a thread wound spirally. The thread is ready to be wound spirally back to the other end where it is tied securely.*

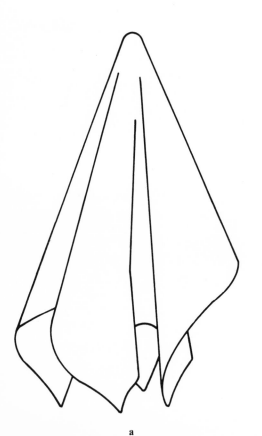

a

b

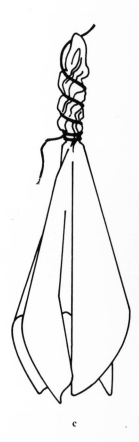

c

3) Lay the third square flat and made guide lines across it with a ruler and pencil or by pulling out single threads at intervals. Then with *even* stitches sew one row straight, one row zigzag, one row in waves. Into the unstitched portion of the cloth you can tie rice grains or barley, spacing evenly to get a spotted effect.

Now boil these samples in any of the strong plant dyes for cotton, such as walnut, or dip them in indigo as described in Chapter 4. Dry them thoroughly before opening the ties.

I shall not give an illustration of the squares untied, but leave beginners the excitement of opening them. From this basic repertory of effects, many different combinations can be planned. Because the dye itself flows a little unevenly, it is necessary to build on a very regular simple foundation, yet each row or tie still will turn out a little different.

It has to be remembered that the outer parts of a length of pleated and tied cloth will absorb more dye than the interior area, but with skill this fact can be used to get even greater variety over the whole piece.

a *A sample piece of cloth stitched up and ready to be gathered, the thread knotted securely with a backstitch.*
b *The same piece of cloth after gathering and fastening.*

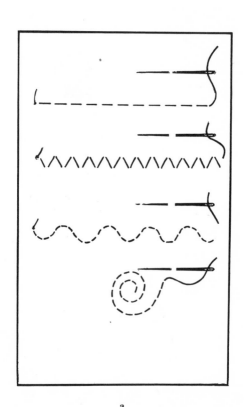

a

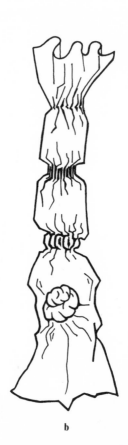

b

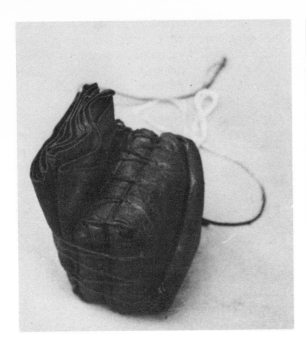

Sequence illustrating the tie-dyeing of a bedspread. The first picture shows the fabric after it has been tied, stitched, and dyed with indigo; the second picture shows the first stage of unwrapping. The third picture shows the next stage of unwrapping: the design is getting lighter where the dye has not penetrated. In the last picture, the complete bedspread is shown, together with student wearing an indigo-tie-dyed shirt.

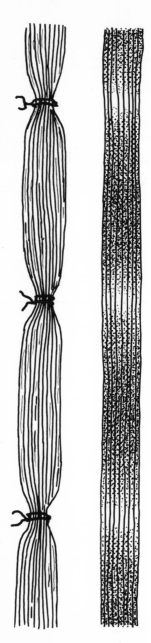

Threads tied to make a tie-dyed warp, and the yarn after it has been dyed and untied.

Into the same dye-pot, for further experimentation, can go hanks of wool and cotton tied along their length in the same way, either at regular intervals or in groups of two ties, then a broader band, or whatever combination you plan. When the skeins are untied, they will have a striped effect that can be used imaginatively in weaving or embroidery, or to produce the patchy effect that seems to be a recurring fashion in knitting.

When you have grasped the principles of tie-dyeing, you can make use of top-dyeing to get a gradation of colors. Thoroughly dry the tied cloth or skeins after their first dyeing. Then you can untie some strings, which means that the original white will take the second color, and make some new ties, which means that here the first color dyed will remain, being blocked from the second color. The rest will take the new color, which will be a combination of the two dyes. It is not nearly so complicated as it sounds. Try it and see!

WARP-DYEING

One traditional way of using tie-dye in the East is warp-dyeing. This produces, because of the slight flooding of the color and the softening effect of the weft mixing with the warp color, a delicate misty pattern.

Beginners who have learned to manipulate the frame loom described earlier will see that by stretching the correct length of warp on two sticks beforehand and securing the ends, they can block out certain parts of this total skein and reassemble it on the loom after dyeing.

Experienced weavers can prepare the warp for the final length of cloth, with every thread in the position it will finally occupy. This warp is then tied into diamond spots or some other very simple pattern and immersed in a dyebath — which needs in this case to be quite large. After dyeing, the warp is then put on the loom with great care to keep it in position, and the weft is woven in. This is usually in the same color, so that where it crosses the undyed areas, the pattern appears in a lighter shade, with hazy edges. This is a skilled craft, for devotees.

New colors are also produced, of course, by the crossing of two sets of colored threads in the warp and the weft. When we remember that the ancient Scottish tartans with their bright orange-reds, plum-purples, yellows, and soft greens were practically all dyed with plants, we can see what infinite variety can be created even in the simplest type of weaving. There is a particular luminosity about the colors created by crossing two contrasting shades: they vibrate in front of our eyes.

Dyers will doubtless use their fibers in other fascinating ways too. The colors of vegetable dyes are on the whole so subtle and varied that if one uses them and gives time and thought to combining them, one develops a subtle color sense that enormously extends the range of colors in a world splashed with crude advertisements and blazing with luminous garments.

9. Planting a Dye Garden

The serious dyer may well want to go on to plant a garden of dye plants. Naturally it is hardly worth sowing those that grow wild nearby and are easily gathered or that seldom grow in sufficient quantities to gather for dyeing. The garden can be planned with narrow paths or steppingstones for easy gathering in any weather. Even without a garden, one can grow potted geraniums and other plants such as marigolds, dahlias, and rudbeckia on a sunny windowsill or balcony, or lily of the valley, ivy, dwarf berberis, or bloodroot on a shady one.

According to the soil and aspect of the ground, it seems best to begin with the plants that grow easily in such conditions and then go on to preparing special plots of differing soils for rarer types. In my own garden in the county of Kent in the south of England, which gets fairly warm summers but quite cold winters, I grow many of the plants discussed in this chapter, and some of them, such as lily of the valley and scarlet geraniums (*Pelargonium* species) give the delight of flowers before I use parts of them for dyes.

In normal loamy soils, an annual that can be planted for immediate use the same year is calliopsis, which produces masses of yellow, crimson, and maroon flowers that give a burnt-orange dye. There are numerous varieties of marigold (*Tagetes*) that yield a dye from the flower heads. Another annual, hardy with us, and a weed that grows in waste places in the United States, soapwort (*Saponaria officinalis*) gives a dye, though not a very firm one. The scent of the soapwort in the evening is a joy, and it attracts the hawk moths that pollinate it. But soapwort and queen of the meadow with its feathery heads both tend to spread and take over the whole bed, so I suggest edging some small plots with brick or stone to keep these within bounds.

Rudbeckia or coneflower, the brown-eyed Susan, grows wild in the United States but is usually grown in its garden varieties in England. It gives a good yellow dye that varies from gold to green according to which part is used and how it is mordanted. With us, it is best sown in autumn for next summer's flowering. The yellow camomile gives a yellow dye. The creeping variety with no flowers will form a green mat in two years; the Elizabethans used it for lawns, which gave a scent when trodden on.

With calliopsis, saponaria, marigold, rudbeckia, and camomile, it is the flower heads that are used, and the gardener is naturally reluctant to pick the large amounts needed, but all these are free-flowering in most districts. Other perennials that grow wild but are pleasant enough to merit garden room are St.-John's-wort, tansy, and goldenrod. The only European species of this last is *Solidago virgaurea,* a rampant yellow plume often seen in cottage gardens. America has dozens of common goldenrods, several of which at least give dyes.

Behind the lower plants can stand the brooms, whose tips have to be cut back after flowering anyway, so you can prune them to use while some are still in flower. Of the same family but giving a firmer dye is dyer's greenwood, which grows well in my shrubbery, being tall enough to catch the sun. In the shrubbery too are the autumn-flaming barberry — I place them well away from paths because of their prickles, but their roots and lower stems yield a good yellow dye. The barberry's reddish berries also provide winter interest, but it is a plant that sucks the ground dry, so plants that need some moisture should not be grown under it.

When my pyracantha bush was knocked down by a falling tree, I tested it and found that the bark yielded a subtle pinkish sand color with chrome.

There are several kinds of privet dye — the view of my neighbor's rubbish dump is blocked out by privet bushes, a useful evergreen yielding a golden dye, but I also grow the yellow-leaved *aurea* variety, which catches any glimpse of the winter sun and gives a fine sharp acid-yellow dye.

The best of the yellow dye plants of the temperate zones is weld, long cultivated commercially for its dye properties in both Europe and the United States. It still grows wild on the chalk downs of southern England, but it seeds itself freely and has to be checked in the garden. It is not very decorative, but its tall spikes are quite handsome.

Yellow can be obtained from many sources, but the salmon-pink to orange-red that we get from pokeberry, though not completely permanent by any method I know, is rare. I have not seen pokeberry growing wild in Britain and a friend who grows it in east Scotland says it suffers from the winters, though it is a common weed in the eastern United States. It was widely used by the early American settlers as a dye, so they may have known some method of making it more permanent.

Mahonia, or Oregon grape, grown decoratively in parks and home gardens in the United States, and in my garden gives a dye from both roots and berries.

Among the few plants that can be grown easily for red is the true dyer's madder, which does not flower until the second or third year but seeds itself around freely, so we need not hesitate to dig up the roots for drying. The French, who were skilled growers before the madder fields of Holland took precedence over them, believed that the parent plant gave the best dye, so the shoots were planted out and left to be taken up some years later. I have found a species of the madder family that gives a pink dye growing wild in the woods of Pennsylvania. Red can also be obtained from bloodroot, native to the United States, but possible to naturalize in Britain. I have it indoors in a pot to enjoy the frail flowers in February, then put it out to spread its red roots during summer. It is hardy in the northern United States; it spreads nicely in half-shady spots which get early sun.

Common wild dye plants, which like well-drained soil and so will often grow in rather stony ground, are the delicate lady's bedstraw (a lesser relation of the true madder) and tall, coarse ragwort. Both ragwort and tansy, with its decorative golden buttons and heavy scent, need sun, and so does the gorse, which flourishes on sandy ground, especially near the sea, but is worth growing only if there is enough space to isolate the prickly stuff. The sight of its occasional yellow flower tips braving the winter is a humorous reminder of the old saying, "When gorse is out of bloom, kissing is out of fashion." Also on poor ground tending towards the sandy will be found saffron crocus. The dye is concentrated in its stigma, but it is more often used in the form of an extract. I have found the colorful spikes of Indian paintbrush *(Castilleja genus)* growing as far north as the Canadian border of the United States, and it is named as an Indian dye, but I had no opportunity to test it. Those who live in sandy districts with hot summers can grow many Indian dye-plants*, including such well-documented ones as the lambs' quarters *(Chenopodium album),* used by the Ojibwa for a green dye, rabbit brush *(Chrysothamnus* species), and osage-orange *(Maclura pomifera),* which I am told is hardy in the northeastern part of the United States but I have not tried it. It is a spiny tree that grows to sixty feet but can be kept trimmed and used as a hedge, but it is not very decorative. Alice Parrit grows her own dyes in New Mexico with unique results.

Few of us would want to encourage bracken, dock or nettles in the garden, but if they have to be pulled up, at least there is some consolation in knowing that they all make a greenish dye. I wish I could say as much for dandelion roots, which are often said to make the magenta of the Scottish kilts, but I have failed to find any way of obtaining this, nor have I met anyone who knows how.

Many gardeners sow vegetables, and if there is a superfluity, spinach and onions are standbys for dyes. Beetroot is disappointing.

Some dyes we get from fruits that may be cultivated for the kitchen — blueberry, huckleberry, mulberry, and blackberry — but I can gather plenty of wild blackberries (or brambles, as they are called in Scotland), that invade the garden. The small wild creeping blackberry of the American West Coast, which makes delicious jam, also gives a good dye from purple to blue. But of course the traditional source of blue is woad, the oldest plant dye known and easy to grow in temperate-climate gardens. In England it is found as an escape from the old woad fields that fell into disuse with the growth of the indigo trade. It grows in poor soil and reaches three feet in height, but its spinach-like plants are hardly decorative and in my garden are relegated to a corner.

*The Denver Museum, Denver, Colorado, publishes two pamphlets on Indian dyes.

There is another group of plants, the heathers, that will grow over a wide area of the land surface if the soil is acid, and this can be provided even in a limestone district like my own by making pockets of peaty soil. I have used the squares between flagstones and old earthenware sinks, forming the sides of steps up and down — so giving a delightful variation of levels — to make such special sites for heathers. These too give color to the autumn and winter garden as well as providing clippings for dye. The carnea heathers will tolerate lime, but I have not found winter clippings from them to yield such a good yellow as the peat heathers.

Those who have a stream or pool are fortunate, for they can grow water-loving plants in natural surroundings. In the lowest corner of the garden, to which the rest drains, you can have a sunk wall or a concrete-lined ditch to trap the water for moisture-loving plants. In my own case I find that the corner with the water butt, which is often overflowing, is always damp and serves well. The water-buttercup or marsh-marigold (*Caltha palustris,* not to be confused with the American garden marigold), which is an early spring plant with bright yellow sun-catching sepals that look like petals, grows wild in water meadows and can be cultivated.

Yet another group that can be specially catered for if one's ground is naturally boggy (and few of us *try* to make a garden in boggy ground) include bog myrtle and bog asphodel, both found wild over miles of Scotland, Ireland, and also the United States, where it is very rare and should not be wantonly collected by dyers.

Another plant that will enhance a boggy patch is the yellow flag iris, with its beautiful flowers. (I have not found that the garden iris, of which I have a great variety, gives a real dye.) The strong black dye is in the rhizome, so it has to be dug up, but these irises are all the better for being divided, and some can be replanted while other pieces are used for dye.

The best of the dye trees are too slow growing for most of us to plant and expect to use in our lifetime. The black walnut, which gives such a strong, lasting dye, will not bear for our generation, and we are fortunate that our forefathers liked the nuts pickled and bequeathed old trees to us.

One fast-growing tree, which I planted to obscure an ugly telephone pole across the road, is the Lombardy poplar. Tall enough to be lopped after four years, it is not a tree to plant near buildings because its roots undermine foundations and crack drains in their search for water.

Other trees that grow fast are the cherries, both the fruiting and the *autumnalis,* which opens its pale pink flowers all winter, even in the snow, and is invaluable for bringing in bud into the house. I have to bark-prune my too swift-growing cherries, and this is an admirable time to get some of the inner bark. Otherwise I watch for tree-felling in the district. Birches are decorative all year and fast growing, but these too need to be far from buildings, for their roots also tend to undermine foundations. The bark of apple and pear trees grown for fruit gives a yellow-brown dye, but one can obtain these colors elsewhere and I would not risk the trees by taking much bark from them. The bark can be obtained from newly felled trees or from lopped branches.

I do not grow the weirdly shaped sumac, a native of North America, because it needs its own space to show it off, but I enjoy my neighbors' and beg berries and young shoots for their dye.

There is one tree that grows vigorously over a large part of the temperate world, seeds itself, is not fussy as to soil, and grows so quickly that one can have the flowers for wine-making and the berries for preserves or dye within four years or so: this is the European elder. I have a large one at my gate and I encourage its self-sown seedlings round the edges of the garden because it scents the yard with its June blossoming and delights the eye from the green spear-buds until the leaves turn yellow and purple in autumn. Its bare winter branches do not block the sun, and its health-giving properties caused an eighteenth-century doctor to get off his horse and bow each time he saw one. It is well known to children wherever it grows because its hollow stems are admirable for pea-shooters, pop guns, and musical pipes. Several of the tree's names reflect this; the Latin name, *sambucus,* is linked to the Greek *sambuke,* a musical pipe and the Scottish name is bore-tree.

Even a small garden can have a part set aside for the basic dye plants, or the whole garden can gradually develop through judicious choice of decorative shrubs into a dye garden. We all of us gather round ourselves the things which are meaningful to us. I work more gladly at routine tasks in the garden because I know that when the foliage has withered, the dyestuffs will be a permanent part of the household. This double association of giving and taking extends our relationship with the plants that share our global environment and multiplies meaning in our life.

List of Suppliers

Suppliers of natural dye materials and chemicals necessary for dyeing are listed below by country. Most drug stores or pharmacies supply basic mordants, and household stores or supermarkets supply the common chemicals such as vinegar, lye, etc. Less common chemicals can be obtained in chemical supply houses for school laboratory materials, which are found in most large cities.

UNITED STATES

Fisher Scientific Co.
52 Fadem Rd.
Springfield, New Jersey

National Biological Supply Co.
2325 Michigan Ave.
Chicago, Illinois 60616

Nature's Herb Co.
281 Ellis St.
San Francisco, California 94012

Spectu-Chem Inc.
1354 Ellison
Louisville, Kentucky 40201

CANADA

Allied Chemical Co. Canada Ltd.
1155 Dorchester Blvd. West
Montreal 2 Quebec
and also
1280 Archibald St., St. Boniface, Manitoba
100 N. Queen St., Toronto 14, Ontario
14505 Edmonton L.D.C. 3, Alberta
Barnet, British Columbia
Port Moody 431, British Columbia
2695 Granville Street, Vancouver, British Columbia

Fisher Scientific Co. Ltd.
P.O. Box 3840, Station D, 14730—115A Ave.
Edmonton, Alberta
and also
184 Railside Rd., Don Mills, Ontario
P.O. Box 1020, 8505 Devonshire Rd., Montreal, Quebec
P.O. Box 2149, 196 West Third Ave., Vancouver 3, British Columbia

World Wide Herbs Ltd.
11 Catherine St. E.
Montreal 129, Quebec

BRITAIN

Comack Chemicals
Swinton Works
Moon St.
London N1

Skilbeck Bros.
55 Glengall St.
London SE 15

Youngs
40 Belvoir
Leicester LEI6QE

AUSTRALIA

C. F. Bailey
St. Aubyn 15 Dutton St.
Bankstown, New South Wales 220

NEW ZEALAND

C.C.G. Industries Ltd.
33 Crowhurst Rd., P.O. Box 3726
New Market, Aukland
and also
411 High St., P.O. Box 3018
Lower Hutt

Bibliography

Asterisks denote books of special importance.

BOOKS ON DYEING

Adrosko, Rita J. *Natural Dyes and Home Dyeing.* New York: Dover, 1971. Formerly titled: *Natural Dyes in the United States.*

Balls, Edward K. *Early Uses of California Plants.* (California Natural History Guides: No. 10). Berkeley: University of California Press, 1962.

Bird, C.L. *The Theory and Practice of Wool Dyeing.* Bradford, Yorkshire: Society of Dyers and Colourists, 1963.

Bolton, Eileen. *Lichens for Vegetable Dyeing.* Newton Centre, Mass.: Charles T. Branford Co., 1960 and London: Studio Books, 1960.

Bryan, Nonabeh G. *Navajo Native Dyes; Their Preparation and Use* (Indian Handcrafts No. 2). Chilocco, 1940.

Creekmore, Betsey B. *Traditional American Crafts.* New York: Hearthside Press, 1968.

*Davenport, Elsie C. *Your Yarn Dyeing; A Book for Handweavers and Spinners.* London: Sylvan Press, 1955.

Davidson, Mary Francis. *The Dyepot.* Gatlinburg, Tenn. 1967.

Duncan, Molly. *Spin Your Own Wool and Dye It and Weave It.* Wellington, New Zealand: A.H. & A.W. Reed, 1968.

Eaton, Allen H. *Handicrafts of the Southern Highlands.* New York: Russell Sage, 1937.

Ellis, Asa. *The Country Dyer's Assistant.* Brookfield, Mass.: E. Merriam & Co., 1798. First book on dyeing published in the United States.

Hurry, J.B. *The Woad Plant.* London: Oxford University Press, 1930.

Kierstead, Sallie P. *Natural Dyes.* Boston: Bruce Humphries, 1950.

Leechman, John Douglas. *Vegetable Dyes from North American Plants.* New York: Hill and Wang (Webb), 1945.

Lesch, Alma. *Vegetable Dyeing: One Hundred and Fifty-One Recipes for Dyeing Yarns and Fabrics with Natural Materials.* New York: Watson-Guptill, 1970.

Lloyd, Joyce. *Dyes From Plants of Australia and New Zealand.* Wellington, New Zealand: A.H. & A.W. Reed, 1968.

Mackenzie. *Five Thousand Recipes.* Pittsburgh: Kay & Troutman, 1846.

Mairet, Ethel M. *Vegetable Dyes,* 5th Ed. Boston: Humphries, 1931 and London: Faber, 1952.

Parslow, V.D. *Weaving and Dyeing Processes in Early New York.* Cooperstown, N.Y.: Farmer's Museum, 1949.

Pope, F. Whipple. *Processes in Dyeing with Vegetable Dyes and Other Means.* Boston: North Bennett Street Industrial School, 1960.

Robinson, Stuart and Patricia Robinson. *Exploring Fabric Printing.* Newton Centre, Mass.: Charles T. Branford, 1970.

*Thurston, V. *The Use of Vegetable Dyes.* Leicester, England: Dryad Press, 1968.

Tidball, Harriet. *Color and Dyeing.* Pacific Grove, Cal.: Craft & Hobby, 1971.

BOOKS ON TEXTILE CRAFTS

Amsden, Charles. *Navaho Weaving, Its Technic and History.* Glorieta, N.M.: Rio Grande, 1964.

Ash, Beryl and Anthony Dyson. *Introducing Dyeing and Printing.* New York: Watson-Guptill, 1970.

Beutlich, Tadek. *Technique of Woven Tapestry.* New York: Watson-Guptill, 1971 and London: Batsford, 1971.

Butler, Anne. *Embroidery for School Children.* Newton Centre, Mass.: Charles T. Branford, 1970 and London: Studio Books, 1971.

Collingwood, Peter. *Techniques of Rug Weaving.* New York: Watson-Guptill, 1969 and London: Batsford, 1968.

Enthoven, Jacqueline. *Stitchery for Children.* New York: Van Nostrand Reinhold, 1968.

Hein, Gisela. *Fabric Printing by Hand: Beginning Techniques.* New York and London: Van Nostrand Reinhold, 1972.

Hartnung, Rolf. *Creative Textile Design.* New York: Van Nostrand Reinhold, 1964 and London: Batsford, 1964.

———. *More Creative Textile Design.* New York: Van Nostrand Reinhold, 1965 and London: Batsford, 1965.

Harvey, Virginia. *Macramé.* New York: Van Nostrand Reinhold, 1967.

Karasz, Mariska. *Adventures in Stitches.* New York: Funk & Wagnalls, 1959.

Krevitsky, Norman. *Batik: Art and Craft.* New York: Van Nostrand Reinhold, 1964.

*———. *Stitchery: Art and Craft.* New York: Van Nostrand Reinhold, 1966.

Liley, Alison. *Embroidery, A Fresh Approach.* London: Mills & Boon.

*Maile, Anna. *Tie-and-Dye as a Present Day Craft.* New York: Ballantine Books, 1971 and London: Mills and Boon, 1963.

McNeill, M. *Pulled Thread.* London: Mills & Boon.

Parker, C. *Inspiration for Embroidery.* London, Batsford.

Proud, Nora. *Introducing Textile Printing.* New York: Watson-Guptill, 1968 and London: Batsford, 1968.

*Rainey, Sarita. *Weaving Without a Loom.* Worcester, Mass.: Davis, 1968.

Seyd, M. *Designing with String.* Plainfield, N.J.: Textile Book, 1969 and London, 1969.

Snook, Barbara. *Needlework Stitches.* New York: Crown, 1972 and London: Batsford, 1972.

Springall, Diana. *Canvas Embroidery.* Newton Centre, Mass.: Charles T. Branford, 1969 and London: Batsford, 1969.

Stratford, M. *Introducing Knitting.* London: Batsford, 1921.

Thomas, Mary. *Mary Thomas's Book of Knitting Patterns.* New York: Dover, 1972.

Tovey, John. *Weaves and Pattern Drafting.* New York: Van Nostrand Reinhold, 1969.

Van Dommelen, David. *Decorative Wall Hangings.* New York: Funk & Wagnalls.

HISTORICAL BOOKS ON PLANTS

Arber, A. *Herbals, Their Origin and Evolution.* New York: Hafner, 1970.

Culpeper, Nicholas. *Culpeper's Complete Herbal.* New York: Sterling, 1959. Culpeper (1616—1654) was a London physician and astrologer whose many books were enormously popular although they were attacked by the established College of Physicians.

Durat, C. *Histoire des Plantes.* Paris, 1605.

Grieve, M. *A Modern Herbal.* New York: Dover, 1967.

Gesner, Konrad von. *Opera Botanica.* London, 1751. Gesner (1516—1565) was a learned German-Swiss writer and naturalist, who illustrated his own works. Although he was best known to his contemporaries as a botanist, his botanical works were not published until the eighteenth century.

Hatton, Richard G. *Handbook of Plant and Floral Ornament from Early Herbals.* New York: Dover, 1960.

Hellot. *The Art of Dyeing.* London, 1789.

Lovell, R. *The Complete Herbal.* London, 1659.

Parkinson, John. *Theatrum Botanicum.* London, 1640. Parkinson (1567—1650) was apothecary to James I and given a title by Charles I for his work in botany. He introduced several new species into England and described 3,800 different plants in his famous herbal.

Rhind, William. *A History of the Vegetable Kingdom.* London: Blackie & Son, 1868.

Turner, W. *Herbal.* London, 1515.

Woodward, Marcus. *Leaves from Gerard's Herbal.* New York: Dover. John Gerard (or Gerarde) (1545—1612) was a surgeon, landscape gardener and "herbalist" to James I of England. His *Herball,* published in London in 1597, was an adaptation of an earlier work, *Stirpium historiae pemptades* (1583) of Rembert Dodoens.

PAMPHLETS AND ARTICLES

Bigham, H. "Dyeing Yarn for Weaving," *School Arts,* Vol. 70 (Feb., 1971).

"Blackburn Workshop," *Handweaver and Craftsman,* Vol. 20, No. 1, (Winter, 1969).

Boydston, K. "Successful Experiment: Michigan Group Explores Natural Dyes," *Handweaver and Craftsman,* Vol. 14, No. 1, (Winter, 1963).

Brewster, Mela S. "A Practical Study of the Use of Natural Vegetable Dyes in New Mexico." University of New Mexico Bulletin, Number 306, May 15, 1937.

Bureau of Indian Affairs, Publications Service, Haskell Indian Junior College, Lawrence, Kansas; various pamphlets.

Cranch, George E. "Unusual Colors from Experiments with Vegetable Dyes," *Handweaver and Craftsman,* Vol. 13, No. 3 (Summer, 1962).

"Dyeing Exhibit," *Handweaver and Craftsman,* Vol. 20, No. 4 (Fall, 1969).

Edelstein, S.M. "Historic Works on Dyeing," *Plants and Gardens,* Vol. 20 (Autumn, 1964). This article is a bibliography.

Fisher, Pat. "Rug Weaving with Natural Dyed Yarns," *Shuttle, Spindle, and Dyepot,* Vol. II, No. 2 (Spring, 1971).

Flynn, E.C. "Make Your Own Dyes from Plants," *Horticulture,* Vol. 49, (September, 1971).

Gerber, Fred and Willie Gerber. "Indigo, Discovery of Plants and Experiments in Dyeing," *Handweaver and Craftsman,* Vol. 19 (Fall, 1968).

————. "Milkweed and Saldunia in the Dyepot," *Handweaver and Craftsman,* Vol. 22, No. 3 (Summer, 1971).

Melvin, A.G. "Dye from Shells," *Hobbies,* Vol. 75 (Fall, 1971).

Robinson, John P. Jr. "Tyrian Purple," *Sea Frontiers,* Vol. 17, No. 2 (April-May, 1971).

*Schetky, Ethel Jane, ed. Dye Plants and Dyeing—A Handbook; from *Plants and Gardens,* Vol. 20, No. 3., Brooklyn Botanical Gardens, 1964.

Society of Apothecaries. Catalogue of Library. London, 1913.

Taggart, Barbara. "Dyepot," *Shuttle, Spindle & Dyepot,* Vol. 2, No. 4 (Fall, 1971).

Whitely, George. "Herbs for Dyeing," New York Times, September 14, 1969.

Woolcot, J. "Ancient Art Revived; Nature as a Source of Pigments in Dyeing Yarns and Fabrics," *Parks and Recreation,* Vol. 1 (Fall, 1966).

Out-of-print and foreign publications can sometimes be obtained from Craft and Hobby Book Service, Big Sur, California, 93920, and K. Drummond Bookseller, 30 Hart Grove Ealing, London W5.

Index of Plants by Color

Yellow, Gold, Orange

Agrimony	yellow-gold
Apple	soft yellow
Barberry	light to strong yellow
Big-Bud Hickory	yellow
Black Oak	gold
Broom	yellow to deep yellow
Broomsedge	yellow
Buckthorn	lemon yellow to bright yellow, old gold (berries); brownish yellow (bark)
Cherry	yellow
Coreopsis	bright yellow to burnt orange
Cotton Flowers	yellow to orange yellow
Dahlia	yellow to bronze-gold
Day Lily	yellow to bright yellow
Dog's Mercury	yellow
Dyer's Greenwood	light to warm yellow
Elder (leaves)	light to deep yellow
Fustic	warm to bright yellow
Geranium	yellow, bronze gold, red-orange
Goldenrod	lemon to tan yellow, gold
Heather	yellow
Hickory	gold to orange
Lady's Bedstraw	yellow
Lily of the Valley	yellow, gold
Lombardy Poplar	khaki, soft yellow, gold
Madder	orange
Madder over yellow	orange to flame
Mahonia (whole plant)	khaki yellow
Marigold	yellow to golden yellow
Mountain Laurel	soft to deep yellow

Oak	yellow, gold, orange
Onion	yellow to brassy orange
Parmelia caperata lichen	yellow to brownish yellow
Parmelia saxatilis lichen	bronze
Pear	soft yellow
Peltigera canina lichen	yellow
Privet (leaves)	dull to bright yellow
Pyracantha	yellow
Queen of the Meadow	greenish yellow
Ragwort	strong yellow
Rudbeckia	greenish yellow, golden yellow (flowers); primrose yellow (whole plant)
Safflower	yellow
St.-John's Wort	medium to buttercup yellow
Silver Birch	yellow (leaves); dull yellow to dull gold (bark)
Smartweed	yellow to gold
Snowberry	shades of yellow
Sweet Gale	yellow
Tansy	yellow
Turmeric	yellow
Usnea barbata lichen	clear yellow
Weld	lemon yellow, golden yellow, orange-yellow
Xanthoria parietina lichen	yellow, tan

Red, Tan, Brown

Alder	yellowish brown
Anchusa	tan, red, purple-red
Big Bud Hickory	tan
Black Walnut	all browns to darkest
Black Willow	rosy tan to warm brown
Bloodroot	red-orange, pinkish red
Buckthorn	brown
Butternut	brown
Cherry	chocolate brown
Cotton Flowers	tan
Cutch	browns
Cypress	bright tan
Dahlia	orange-red
Evernia prunastri lichen	brown
Geranium	tan to red-orange
Hemlock	rose-tan
Hypogymnia psychodes lichen	golden brown
Lady's Bedstraw (roots)	red, light orange-red, purplish red
Larch	brown
Lobaria pulmonaria lichen	brown
Mountain Laurel	gray-brown
Madder	red, orange-red
Mahonia (roots)	tan, buff to brown
Menegussia pertusa lichen	deep reddish brown
Norway Maple	pinkish tan
Oak	brown
Ochrolechia parella lichen	orange-red
Osage-Orange	yellow-tan
Parmelia omphalodes lichen	red-brown
Pokeweed	red to soft tan
Prickly-Pear Cactus	rose-red to tan
Pyracantha	pinkish brown

Sloe	—red-brown
Sumac	warm tan, brown
Umbilicaria pustulata lichen	bright red

Blue, Purple, Rose, Pink

Bilberry	pink to purple
Black Currant	deep lilac to purple
Black Huckleberry	shades of purple
Blackberry	gray-purple (young shoots); rose (berries)
Cladonia impexa lichen	soft pink
Cochineal	pink to scarlet, gray-purple
Cochineal over blue	purple
Elder (berries)	violet
Evernia prunastri lichen	plum purple
—Indigo	pale blue to navy blue
Logwood	violet to purple
Mahonia (berries)	purplish blue
Menegussia pertusa lichen	soft pink
Ochrolechia tartarea	red-purple
Privet (berries)	pale pink to blue-purple
Roccella tinctoria lichen	purple
Silver Birch (bark)	purple
Sloe	rose-pink
Usnea lirta lichen	purple
Wild Grape Vine	lavender to reddish purple
Woad	pale to deep blue
Xanthoria parietina lichen	purple-red, blue

Green

Bracken	yellow-green, lime green
Butternut	green
Cutch	green
Day Lily	blue-green
Fustic	olive green
Goldenrod	yellow-green
Horsetail	green
Indigo over yellow	green
Ivy	yellow-green
—Lily of the Valley	soft apple green
Nettle	yellow-green to gray-green
Privet (leaves)	green to dark green
Queen of the Meadow	green
Ragwort	strong yellow
Rudbeckia (flower heads)	green
Weld	olive

Gray, Black

Alder	black
Anchusa	gray
Blackberry (young shoots)	gray to near black

Bracken	gray
Buckthorn (berries)	blue-gray
Butternut	gray
Cutch	gray to black
Elder (bark)	gray
Ivy	greenish-gray
Logwood	gray to near black
Mountain Laurel	gray
Sumac	gray
Wild Grape Vine	purplish gray
Yellow Flag Iris	black

Index of Dye Recipes by Plant Common Name

Note: The recipe for Cochineal may be found on page 74

Index of Dye Recipes by Plant Botanical Name

Note: The recipe for Cochineal may be found on page 74

Index of Dye Recipes by Plant Botanical Name

Table of Measures

Weight

1 ounce (oz) equals 28.349 grams (g), and 1 pound (lb) equals .453 kilograms (kg), but for our purposes the following rough equivalents are practical:

1 oz = 30 g
½ lb = 250 g
1 lb = .5 kg
2 lb = 1 kg

It is only in the measurements of chemicals that one needs even this degree of accuracy. Whenever possible, measures are given in American teaspoons (tsp) or tablespoons (tbsp) as well.

Volume

The British gallon, or Imperial gallon, contains 4 Imperial (40-ounce) quarts; the American gallon contains 4 quarts of 32 ounces each. I have found this to be just enough for dyeing 4 ounces of wool, but Americans should use a generous gallon. The British cup is 10 fluid ounces; the American is 8 fluid ounces. Because American and British liquid measures are different, I have tried to avoid using fluid ounces and multiples thereof. I have, where possible, used teaspoons and tablespoons, and so give their fluid-ounce equivalents here:

1 tsp = 1/6 fl oz (1 European coffee spoon)
1 tbsp = 1/2 fl oz (1 European soup spoon)
2 tbsp = 1 fl oz

For dry measure, I have given quantities in quarts (qts) and pecks (pks); the difference between the American and British is so slight that I have not distinguished between them.

I have totally ignored the metric liters, but for the convenience of dyers using the metric system, the following equivalents may be used:

1 fl oz = 30 cc
1 gal = 4½ liters
1 qt (dry measure) = 1 liter
1 pk = 9 liters